D1301948

"For every soul who has felt the loss of life through miscarriage or the absence of hope that accompanies infertility, *Finding Hope After Miscarriage* by Karen Edmisten offers a wellspring of grace. Filled both with the voices of those who have experienced this sacrificial love and with helpful resources full of practical insights, Karen's book will be a gift of compassion and healing for many."

—Lisa M. Hendey, author of *A Book of Saints for Catholic Moms* and founder of CatholicMom.com

"Any mother who has suffered the loss that is miscarriage knows just how empty her arms and heart can feel. When I lost my first baby, it felt as if my insides had been scooped out, leaving nothing behind but a sun-scraped void. If only I'd had a resource like *Finding Hope After Miscarriage* to help me to fill my emptiness! Karen Edmisten has written a wise and beautiful book that delivers just what the title says. This gentle companion gifts hurting mothers and their loved ones with both practical and spiritual wisdom to help them find hope and healing in the wake of a great loss. *Finding Hope After Miscarriage*, a must-read for anyone who has been touched by miscarriage, would also be a valuable guide for someone who is seeking to minister to a mother who has lost a baby.

"In this treasure of a book, Catholic convert Karen Edmisten not only shares her own experience with multiple miscarriages—the entries from her journal are so filled with honesty, hurt, anguish, and hope, they read like prayerful psalms—but includes as well stories from other women who have lost babies. These women's unique voices delicately probe the myriad emotions that the loss of a miscarriage brings to a mother and her family. Their honest words beautifully convey the ache-all-over kind of longing for a child whom they will never know on this earth. They also reveal the glimmer of God's hope that shines through the suffering. By sharing their pain, Edmisten and her contributors give other women permission to mourn their babies in a world that might discount a tiny, new life. This deeply moving account of loss, suffering, grace, and redemption has the power to open the door of the reader's soul to God and his healing grace."

—Kate Wicker, author of *Weightless: Making Peace With Your Body* and
Catholic Digest columnist

"This lovely and sorely needed book will powerfully and tenderly touch your soul with abiding comfort and blessing. I highly recommend it for mothers who have miscarried as well as for family members, priests, deacons, religious, Catholic medical staff, and those in ministry."

—Donna-Marie Cooper O'Boyle, bestselling author of numerous books,
including *Embracing Motherhood,* is a TV host on EWTN
and a mother of five on earth and three in heaven

AFTER MISCARRIAGE

A Catholic Woman's Companion
to Healing and Hope

Karen Edmisten

servant
AN IMPRINT OF
FRANCISCAN MEDIA
Cincinnati, Ohio

LIBRARY OF CONGRESS CATALOGING-IN-PUBLICATION DATA
Edmisten, Karen.
Finding hope after miscarriage : a companion in grief and healing, hope, and prayer / Karen Edmisten.
p. cm.
Includes bibliographical references (p.   ) and index.
ISBN 978-0-86716-997-3 (pbk. : alk. paper) 1. Consolation. 2. Miscarriage—Religious aspects—Christianity. 3. Premature infants—Death—Religious aspects—Christianity. 4. Bereavement—Religious aspects—Christianity. I. Title.
BV4907.E36 2012
242'.4—dc23
                                   2011046100

ISBN 978-0-86716-997-3

Published by Servant, an imprint of Franciscan Media
28 W. Liberty St.
Cincinnati, OH 45202
www.FranciscanMedia.org

For Tom,
the father of my many children
in heaven and on earth.

Contents

ACKNOWLEDGMENTS

As I worked on this book, friends often asked if it was painful to revisit my own miscarriages and to hear so many other stories of loss.

"No," I said, "not exactly painful. I've been blessed with great healing, and I've grown closer to the Lord with every step. I have enough 'distance' to handle it."

Then one day as I sifted through mementos, journals, cards, and letters, I found myself sobbing. Though working on the manuscript wasn't painful in precisely the way people guessed, it was extremely emotional.

But I'll take that kind of emotion any day. I'll thank God for it too, because it is a reaction born of sacrificial love and the recognition that suffering has meaning. It's an acknowledgment of the beauty of the body of Christ. And it's the kind of emotion that has nowhere to turn but to the foot of the cross. "Not my will, but yours, be done" (Luke 22:42). Such pain accepts this fallen world but looks forward to the glory of the next.

And so the answer to "Was this a hard book to write?" is that, yes, it was hard. But it was also glorious. These stories—from men and women willing to share how fiercely they love the babies they lost—are powerful, life affirming, and overflowing with God's goodness.

The eternal souls the Lord allowed me the privilege of carrying in my womb have enriched my life immeasurably. As hard as it was to believe at one time, I would not change a thing. Thank you, Jesus. And thank you to all of my children and to my beloved husband.

"My yoke is easy, and my burden is light," Jesus tells us (Matthew 11:30). And so it is. Even when it's hard.

Thank you to the many mothers and fathers who shared their stories with me: Johnna Miller, Charlotte W., R., Elisabeth and Joshua, Roxane Salonen, Sue Umezaki, Karen Murphy Corr, Melanie Bettinelli, Sara Lewis Holmes, Margaret Berns, B., Ellen Gable Hrkach, Janet Brungardt, Jolene, Mary DeTurris Poust, Abigail Benjamin, and those who wished to remain anonymous. I am grateful for your generosity in sharing your babies with me. You, your children, and your words are gifts.

I'm extremely grateful to Karen Murphy Corr for pointing me to George MacDonald's *Diary of an Old Soul*. I think of myself as a MacDonald fan, but this book was not in my collection. Thank you, Karen.

Thanks to Tony Beardslee for allowing me to reprint an excerpt of his song "Pair of Wings." (You can read more about the song's origin and listen to it online at www.tonybeardslee.com/My Music/Volume 1.) Thanks to Danae and to Matt and Maria. And thank you to my spiritual advisors and friends, Fr. Joe Taphorn and Fr. Scott Hastings.

Thank you to Cindy Cavnar and Servant for saying yes to this project, and thanks to Louise Paré, Claudia Volkman, Lucy Scholand, and Nicholas Frankovich for seeing it through to completion in the midst of a number of changes.

INTRODUCTION

> No one ever told me that grief felt so like fear. I am not afraid,
> but the sensation is like being afraid. The same fluttering in
> the stomach, the same restlessness, the yawning. I keep on
> swallowing.
>
> —C.S. Lewis, *A Grief Observed*[1]

I was in a store; I don't even remember which one. The wife of my husband's boss, a woman I barely knew, was in the same aisle. She said something cordial: "Why, hello! Mrs. Edmisten, isn't it? How are you?"

I wanted to say, "I'm just fine, thanks. How are you?" But I was not fine, and I couldn't seem to hide that fact from anyone. I burst into tears.

It wasn't the first time that after a miscarriage I couldn't control my emotions in public. One of the most overwhelming moments of my life was when we discovered that we had lost our first baby. Fifteen weeks into the pregnancy, we had an ultrasound and found that the baby had actually died weeks before. I fell apart, sobbing.

When it was time to leave the doctor's office, a nurse showed me a back door, saying it would offer me more privacy and be less difficult than walking through the waiting room. But later I wondered if she'd shielded other patients from me because I was a keening madwoman.

My child had died. I didn't know how to act.

Hannah's Tears

When we're mourning we don't always want words. We know that no list of facts or level of wisdom will lessen our pain. There's no solution to the loss, no correction of the course that will help us arrive at a different destination. All we really want is a friend who will sit with us and let us be what we are: sad. Let us feel what we're feeling: pain. Let us do what we need to do: cry. We want to get beyond the pain and discomfort and move on. But before we can genuinely heal, we have to slog through some misery.

There is a healing apostolate in my parish for those who have miscarried. We named it the Hannah Ministry after the tears Hannah shed in her barrenness: "She was deeply distressed and prayed to the Lord, and wept bitterly" (1 Samuel 1:10). I suggested this name at the ministry's outset but then wondered if the reference was too negative. In focusing on grief, would we seem dismissive of the hope of the resurrection of the body?

Others felt that adopting Hannah's name was appropriate. Both her intense desire for children and her grief in barrenness were intimately connected to her relationship with the Lord. She turned to God with every thought, desire, fear, and plea. When she fervently wished for the elusive gift of a baby, she said, "I have been pouring out my soul before the LORD.... I have been speaking out of my great anxiety and vexation" (1 Samuel 1:15, 16). God the Father was part of Hannah's journey every step of the way.

Hannah felt the absence of children deeply. Her infertility absorbed her and forced her, in a sense, to pray her way through the experience. Eventually she did bear a child, her beloved son Samuel, and she went on to have five more children. So our group's name, the Hannah Ministry, certainly hints at hope for the future.

Of course, not every childless woman who pleads with the Lord will ultimately have children, but that isn't the point. The real point lies in Hannah's feelings and her trust in the Lord. Although her trust didn't waver, she wept bitterly over what God had allowed her to endure. Hannah had to sit with her grief when it was the crushing reality of her life.

And so these pages are for every Hannah who has ever wept over the loss of a child or the absence of fertility. I hope these words can sit with you as you trek through the days (or weeks, months, or years) of mourning. I pray that this little book can be a compassionate companion for you as you pour your soul out to the Lord.

But I also hope that such grief isn't the final station on your journey. Bitter weeping, however necessary to deal with the emotions God gave us, is not an end. It is the means to an end. Grief is necessary, and our children deserve the dignity of our mourning, the recognition of their infinite worth, the respect that is manifest in our grieving their passing. Yet the Lord doesn't want us to live in the dwelling place of affliction forever.

If tears are the means, moving forward in love is the end toward which we work. It is agonizing work indeed. But the torment of the cross eventually leads us to a resurrection: an ability to thank God for the gifts that are our children, whom we had to let go of much too soon, and to release them to our good and loving Lord. The "fluttering in the stomach, the restlessness, the yawning" will not be our lifelong companions. We can trust in His merciful promises.

> Now I am setting out into the unknown. It will take me a long while to work through the grief. There are no shortcuts; it has to be gone through.
>
> —Madeleine L'Engle, *Two-Part Invention: The Story of a Marriage*[2]

Wading Through the Grief
From Johnna

The physical part is over. With seven other children to care for, I have to move on. I seem to be the only one thinking of our baby, Samuel. Why doesn't everyone feel as I do? I cry whenever I'm alone.

A month later: For Christmas my husband gives me a beautiful statue of a little boy being cradled in the hands of God. The kids yell, "It's Samuel!" I cry.

I go out with a friend. She lets me just talk. She understands and listens! And listens, and listens…

I talk with Father W. and work through some past issues as well. I wouldn't have done this if Samuel hadn't been in my life. He's given me courage and strength.

Fast forward three years. A friend has miscarried. It hits me hard, and I tear up while making Sunday brunch. When my husband asks what's wrong, I tell him about our friend's loss. He asks why it's bothering me, and I explode, yelling at him for not understanding, not caring, not being there, not even thinking about Samuel. He is stunned. He had no idea how I felt.

I had no idea how I felt. The tears come, fast and furious. Mark holds me and lets me cry for a long time.

We talk about how to commemorate Samuel Augustine, and on the feast of Our Lady of Guadalupe, a Mass is said in his memory. I finally have closure.

We still talk about our saint in heaven, and we know he's praying for each of us. We "count" him: We have nine children instead of the eight everyone can see. (Our kids even count him as "number eight" when we do a head count.) Acknowledging Samuel, no matter how short his time with us was, has become an important part of our lives. I still cry, but not as often, and the tears are tears of love and hope rather than of sadness.

In Samuel, God blessed me with a gift that I will always remember, because he grew under, and into, my heart.[3]

· · ·

Did You Know?

Having Mass said in memory of the child you lost is a holy and healing act. A "memorial Mass" is what you can request. You may also want to find out if your parish offers an annual Mass for parents who have lost children. Talk to your priest to find out more and make arrangements.

Notes From My Journal

"Karen, your pregnancy is not progressing as it should be."

I've been walking around in a daze of grief and disbelief. On Thursday they told us that our baby stopped developing. They never said "died." But that is what they assume, and that is what they meant, although nothing has been done yet. I am still carrying the baby, my body still thinks I am pregnant.

When we left the doctor's office, I felt such intense misery—deeper, harsher, more painful than I knew I could feel. I wanted to shriek at the world, at God, at the doctors, and I wanted to know why. I finally screamed, "This is not fair!"

I'm afraid of the depth of my feeling. I'm afraid that if I dive into it completely, I'll never come back up.

One of my prenatal books said it's rare to not physically lose the baby when he or she dies, but apparently I fall into the "rare" category. I am waiting, waiting… Everything's scary right now and upside down. The world feels like a dangerous place…

People say, "It's for the best—you'll have another," but they don't understand. It may be true, but that isn't what's important now. Right now I am grieving the loss of this baby—the one that was conceived in April, that would have been born in January. The one I pictured myself pregnant with at Christmas. The baby we'd have had a shower for in August with friends. This baby.

I can't pretend this baby never existed or cover the pain with optimism. I know optimism will come, but right now my baby, this baby, is dead, and I have to mourn. It's not that the babies to come don't matter. It's just that they aren't this baby.

There's no evidence of it, but I'm a mother.

> Will there really be a "Morning"?
> Is there such a thing as "Day"?
> Could I see it from the mountains
> If I were as tall as they?
>
> . . .
>
> Oh, some Scholar! Oh, some Sailor!
> Oh, some Wise Men from the skies!
> Please to tell a little Pilgrim
> Where the place called "Morning" lies!
>
> —Emily Dickinson[4]

Number the Stars

From a mother who experienced multiple miscarriages

When does life begin?

Conception, of course.

When does life begin to be important, memorable, meaningful, sacred, worth grieving over?

Conception.

We didn't tell many people. First, I was embarrassed about miscarrying again after all the effort, time, and money we had put into trying to correct the problem. Part of this comes from a fleeting feeling of inadequacy, wondering if it's not a medical problem at all but rather "all in my head." Second, I didn't want people to feel sorry for me. Third, I didn't want to talk about it. And fourth, did I have grounds to grieve about it? After all, it happened so early.

After wading through thoughts about what defines human life and its importance at all stages, I realized that my child is a person with a body and soul, now with God in heaven. We cocreated new life with God. Even though he lived only a few days or weeks and his life may have been destined to fail from the beginning, we did add another soul to God's people, to help His children "number the stars" (Genesis 15:5).[5]

Did You Know?

Sometimes there appears to be no reason for a miscarriage. In other cases there may be medical reasons worth investigating. For example, after some testing following my second loss, my doctor determined that I needed progesterone supplementation with subsequent pregnancies.

D&Cs (dilation-and-curettage procedures) were necessary with all of my miscarriages, and after my last two losses we discovered that the babies had trisomy 16, a chromosome abnormality that nearly always results in miscarriage. There was nothing we could have done differently.

My doctor was a faithful, pro-life Catholic. My D&Cs were performed only after both ultrasounds and blood tests (which showed declining HCG, or pregnancy hormone, levels) confirmed that my babies had already died. It was helpful and comforting to know that my doctor and I shared the same perspective on the sanctity of life. If you need help finding a pro-life doctor or are looking for other medical support, there are resources available. (See the appendix for a starting point.)

> I am your Saviour. Not only from the weight of sin, but from
> the weight of care, from misery, and depression, from want and
> woe, from faintness and heartache. Your Saviour.
> —A.J. Russell, *God Calling*[6]

Notes From My Journal

It's touching and sad that it never occurred to Tom that this could happen. I worried about miscarriage in the way that every pregnant woman worries: not believing it would happen to me but aware that it was possible. Tom thought of a miscarriage as something that happens after a fall, as in an old movie. It never occurred to him that one day we could walk unsuspecting into the doctor's office and be told that something was horribly wrong.

I have felt myself slowly coming back to life these last few days. There are still tears and waves of grief, but I also feel the awakening of healing.

Today we went to meet the couple we'll be renting the house from. When we were introduced, the woman said, "Oh! I thought you were expecting a baby!"

"We lost it," I said simply. I blinked back tears, handling it better than I thought I could. The horrible, awkward silence passed, and we stepped inside to look at the house.

> Hope in God; for I shall again praise him,
>   my savior and my God.
>
> —Psalm 42:5

BLESSED BE GOD FOREVER
From Charlotte W.

My husband tells the story of a Franciscan priest who was desperately running to catch a bus. He made it up the steps just before the doors closed behind him. Then he plopped down exhausted, proclaiming, "God is good!" A little old lady sitting next to him smiled and said, "Yes, and He would be just as good if you hadn't caught the bus!"

What is it about our fallen human nature that rejoices in His goodness only when things go our way? An unexpected refund arrives in the mail…God is good! A friend shows up with a plate of cookies…God is good!

Cookies or not, God is always good. Today especially, I will try to remember that God is good. In spite of tragedy and sadness, God is good. In spite of losing a little one whose face we will not know this side of heaven, God is good. In spite of still carrying that tiny heart that we never had the pleasure of watching beat, God is good.

In light and in shadow, in sunshine and in rain…
in heartbreak…

in sorrow…

in pain…

God is good. Blessed be God forever.[7]

• • •

Praise the LORD!

Praise the LORD, O my soul!

I will praise the LORD as long as I live;

I will sing praises to my God while I have being.

—Psalm 146:1–2

Did You Know?

It's tricky deciding when to announce a pregnancy. Some people prefer to keep the news quiet until all the first-trimester fears have passed. On the other hand, there can be beauty and benefit in announcing the news early and asking friends and family for prayers.

When I was pregnant with Raphael (who would be our fifth loss), we asked for prayers from everyone we knew. Later, after we lost the baby, a friend and his wife said that praying for our child had been a gift to them. After expressing his deep sympathy, Matt wrote:

Despite the sadness, I do find consoling thoughts. Amazingly, in a very short life, Baby E. became a true epicenter of prayer.

To live such a short time without sinning while fueling so much prayer is the stuff of saints. I wish I could claim such a legacy. Of course, none of this would have been possible if Baby E.'s mother had not shared her child with us, and for this I will always be grateful.

When you ask others for their prayers, you are reaching into and acting as part of the body of Christ. What a gift.

Notes From My Journal

Another coworker (who hadn't heard that I miscarried) congratulated me today, and I handled it by bursting into tears. Will I ever be able to handle it? It's such an intimate thing, and yet I keep telling everyone about it, even those who didn't know I was pregnant to begin with. Maybe death is like that—so intimate but so terribly public as well.

Arguably, the death of my baby could remain intimate. It was never fully public, in a sense. But that isn't really true either. As long as I go out in public, as long as I talk to and interact with others, I carry the pain and the death of my child with me.

I could no more pretend that nothing has happened than I could pretend to be fine if my husband died.

Bringing Good Out of Grief
From R.

My miscarriage happened at home. It was the most painful thing, physically and emotionally, that I have ever been through. When it was over, after eight miserable hours, I held our tiny baby in the palm of my hand. My husband and I wondered what to do next. This baby had had a beating heart. This baby was a person, a human being, our child.

We called our parish for direction. We had so many questions: Do we bury the baby? How? Where? Is there a right or wrong way, or place, for such a burial? What are the Catholic Church's rules on this? We needed comfort and sympathy, but we also needed information and clear guidance. A miscarriage is a death, and we needed to know how to proceed.

I thought if anyone could understand and comfort us, it was the Catholic Church. We stand with the Church in her strong and absolute respect for life. Sadly, the resources offered to us were scant. There just wasn't anything formally in place at our parish to offer the kind of guidance we sought (though the priest we contacted was kind and compassionate).

With the blessing and help of that same priest, I started a new group in my parish. My hope is that through the Catholic Church and the efforts of individual parishes, we can make the aftermath of miscarriage a little more bearable for women. We need to be there for families and to offer help. Our group is working to offer women the information they need. I want the next woman who calls her priest with this sad news to hang up the phone feeling comforted and reassured. I want her to know that she has options about what to do next.[8]

· · ·

Did You Know?

You have the right to make your wishes known, both to your doctor and your parish. Ask whatever questions you need to have answered. For example, you can inquire about what will happen during and after a D&C. You can ask about your baby's remains. (You may have to inquire about state laws.) You may ask for a copy of a pathology report. You can ask your priest about talking to a local funeral home. Many funeral homes offer free or reduced-cost services for infants, even when lost through early miscarriage.

No community is perfect. Unfortunately, not every doctor's office or parish is fully informed about what a Catholic woman can or may want to do during and after a miscarriage. If your local support is not as helpful as you had hoped, there are other resources available to you. (Please see resources section on page 125 for a list of support organizations.)

Perhaps the Lord is even calling you to start something in your parish or diocese to help other women?

Nothing is small in the service of God.

—St. Francis de Sales[9]

He Knew Nothing but Love
From Elisabeth

Christopher has been an important part of our lives and always will be. Since we lost him, we've been able to visit his gravesite nearly every weekend, which has been so healing.

Our archdiocese offers a free funeral Mass, burial, and gravesite for all children. The staff were amazing to work with. They even made prayer cards for Christopher. Perhaps not every diocese offers this, but it meant so much to our family. We were amazed by the loving service.

The most meaningful words spoken at the time of our loss came from the priest at Christopher's funeral. He said, "Christopher knew nothing but love." That has remained with me in my daily prayer since we lost our little baby boy. This is every parent's dream, that our children will know nothing but love. I found myself smiling—so happy that we'd done what was asked of us. We are still saddened that we could not keep him but joyful too, knowing that we reached our goal with one of our children.

During our night prayers, the kids still say good night to Christopher and blow him kisses. We know he is our advocate in heaven. We have an ultrasound picture of him next to our family picture. We hang a stocking for him at Christmas; we put a cross with flowers in our yard, commemorating him. Through our loss our family has been blessed in tremendous ways. It has brought us closer together.

Each time we visit his gravesite, the kids bring him a new toy, flowers, or a pinwheel. They love to visit after Sunday Mass, because with this come juice and donuts—what gets better than that? We can celebrate as a family, both here and in heaven!

My hope is that our children will know more about the goodness of God as a result of our instilling in them this love for Christopher. They have learned about death. We're trying to capture it in a way that is not full of fear but full of life and a better understanding of what we were made for. At the age of four, our daughter knows that she has a brother in heaven she can pray to. That is pretty cool.

Joshua, my husband, has always been good to remind me that "this is God's baby first." We have all of our children on loan; with our miscarriage we learned how precious life is, how important to remember our many blessings. There will always be elements of sadness in losing Christopher, but so much healing has taken place, and Joshua was instrumental in that. He's always been a good listener, but after our loss he knew how important it was for me to talk. This has been key to our growth in love—grieving together.[10]

. . .

In this you rejoice, although now for a little while you may have to suffer through various trials, so that the genuineness of your faith, more precious than gold that is perishable even though tested by fire, may prove to be for praise, glory, and honor at the revelation of Jesus Christ.

—1 Peter 1:6–7, *NAB*

Did You Know?

There are many ways to commemorate the life of your child. Although it may seem that there's not a lot to save after a miscarriage, I found a number of things.

I was always so excited to be pregnant that I saved my positive pregnancy tests, reminders that my babies had lived, however briefly. Booklets on grieving, given to me by my obstetrician after our losses, bear the names of my lost children. Cards of congratulations for the pregnancies and sympathy cards for the miscarriages are carefully tucked into a box of memories of our saints in heaven.

Ideas from others include making a donation to your favorite charity in your baby's name and, every year on the date of his birth into heaven, commemorating the event with a prayer, a special meal, or just some quiet time. Rosaries and jewelry containing birthstones or names are also options. Other ideas: planting a tree or favorite flower, designing or buying a wall hanging with the baby's name on it, writing a letter or poem to your child.

And don't forget to ask your baby to pray for you. Our children are powerful intercessors in heaven!

Empty Arms in God's Hands
From Roxane Salonen

At eleven weeks pregnant, we learned our third baby had died. We were ill prepared to deal with our shock and deep sadness over the unexpected loss. We turned to Fr. Tim.

A few days before his visit, my husband and I discussed whether we should name our child. Fr. Tim would offer a formal prayer for our baby; it seemed fitting to have a name for this soul, a human being, a family member.

We decided to name our baby Gabriel, which means "devoted to God." Although our baby's gender was unknown, I had felt strongly that I was carrying a boy, and this was a name we'd contemplated specifically for this child. It seemed doubly appropriate given that Gabriel is the angel who appeared to Mary with news of a small, special being in her womb.

The day of Fr. Tim's visit, I gathered up some mementos (cards we'd received congratulating us on our pregnancy, a gift from a friend, some e-mail messages). I placed these in a box decorated with angels and roses and named it "Gabriel's Box." This marked the beginning of my healing.

Fr. Tim next led an impromptu ceremony that included a blessing with holy water and prayers for our baby, for the integrity of our marriage, and for pregnant couples in our lives. He led songs of loss, life, and hope. Because singing always has been an emotional experience for me, I was unable to join in, knowing I would break down. But the strength I gained in hearing these two men in song, each with an arm on my shoulder, was powerful and uplifting. It let me internalize my loss and cry out my anguish without feeling alone.

The prayers also were immeasurably cleansing. This was the first time since the miscarriage that I'd allowed myself a face-to-face encounter with God. In a final petition, I was able to pray for our baby and ask God to take him into His hands and nurture him until we are able to see him in heaven.

We are thankful that so early in the grieving process we discovered a precious gift left by little Gabriel. Never before had we looked toward heaven with such eagerness. Knowing our entry there someday would unite us with the baby we never held gave us new vision and comfort.[11]

· · ·

Did You Know?

Many parents wonder about the fate of their miscarried, unbaptized children. Please don't worry about your baby's salvation. Do not fret that you were unable to baptize your baby before he died. Baptism is a sacrament for the living. And you need not worry about limbo (which has never been an official doctrine of the Church but rather was a theological supposition).

As the Church teaches us, our God is good and merciful. He loves our babies even more than we are able, and the best thing we can do is to place all our trust and hope in Him. The Catechism of the Catholic Church says: "God has bound salvation to the sacrament of Baptism, but he himself is not bound by his sacraments" (*CCC,* #1257).

In other words, God gives us the rules ("Baptism is necessary for salvation") because we need them, but He can "break" His own rules. He knows about our miscarriages, our desires, our hopes, and our hearts. He knows our pain, and He knows that our babies did not have a chance to live outside the womb. Trust our loving Father.

You can always turn to your priest for help. Ask him to pray for you and with you. You may want to ask him for a blessing, such as this one from the *Book of Blessings*:

> For those who trust in God,
> in the pain of sorrow there is consolation,
> in the face of despair there is hope,
> in the midst of death there is life.

[Parents], as we mourn the death of your child, we place ourselves in the hands of God and ask for strength, for healing, and for love.

. . .

Compassionate God,
soothe the hearts of [these parents],
and grant that through the prayers of Mary,
who grieved by the cross of her Son,
you may enlighten their faith,
give hope to their hearts,
and peace to their lives.
Lord,
grant mercy to all the members of this family
and comfort them with the hope
that one day we will all live with you,
with your Son Jesus Christ, and the Holy Spirit,
for ever and ever.

　　—Order for the Blessing of Parents After a Miscarriage[12]

If you are close to your pastor, asking for his help may feel natural to you. If you've never invited a priest to your home, however, you might feel a little awkward. Don't worry. Our priests are here to minister to us, not only during Holy Mass and for the sacramental milestones in our families' lives but in all the circumstances and crosses we encounter and carry. Our Catholic faith can help us to grieve both formally, through liturgy and prayer, and informally, through the fatherly love of our priests.

. . .

Notes From My Journal

Overwhelmed by depression, feeling empty and unpregnant and robbed.

Sometimes I feel bitter toward every woman who easily, unthinkingly carries a pregnancy to term. I wonder when such bitterness will go away.

Last night, when I so strongly felt the stab of our loss, I cried out to God. "Why? Why did this happen? What am I supposed to learn?" I wanted—demanded—a reason. Then I thought about how I constantly talk to God but rarely listen for His voice. So I lay still and did my best to clear my mind of questions and simply listen. And eventually a picture came to my mind.

I was weeping, and Jesus approached me, held me, a bloody, wounded hand on my hair, a strong arm around me. He said that He would not tell me why but that He knew what I felt.

And even in our sleep pain that cannot forget, falls drop by drop upon the heart, and in our own despite, against our will, comes wisdom to us by the awful grace of God.

—Aeschylus[13]

If the clouds are full of rain,
    they empty themselves on the earth;
and if a tree falls to the south or to the north,
    in the place where the tree falls, there it will lie.
He who observes the wind will not sow;
    and he who regards the clouds will not reap.

As you do not know how the spirit comes to the bones in the womb of a woman with child, so you do not know the work of God who makes everything.

In the morning sow your seed, and at evening withhold not your hand; for you do not know which will prosper, this or that, or whether both alike will be good.

—Ecclesiastes 11:3–6

A Healing Season

From Sue Umezaki

I went to the cabin and planted lily bulbs. A remembrance. Our little baby who is with Jesus—I will think of him as my Lily, though I don't know if the baby was a girl or a boy. Next summer I will breathe the lilies' fragrance and thank God that He is all-sufficient.[14]

· · ·

Remember, O most gracious Virgin Mary, that never was it known that anyone who fled to thy protection, implored thy help, or sought thine intercession was left unaided. Inspired by this confidence, I fly unto thee, O Virgin of virgins, my mother; to thee do I come, before thee I stand, sinful and sorrowful. O Mother of the Word Incarnate, despise not my petitions, but in thy mercy hear and answer me. Amen.

Notes From My Journal

My second miscarriage…

The grief is different this time. There is a numbness, a sickening feeling. This pain is all too familiar. Tears, but of a different quality. Innocence lost, I guess.

I kept asking God to forgive me for feeling fear, not trusting Him completely. But I couldn't deny the blood, or that the nausea had left me. I couldn't ignore that somehow, subtly, in my breasts and my abdomen, I had been feeling less pregnant than before. I was not surprised when I saw the baby on the ultrasound screen, its heart still and silent.

When we left the doctor's office, we walked out the back door—the same door through which I exited last time, wailing—down a crooked path by the side of the building. A route from his office that should not be familiar to us but is.

After the D&C:

I miss our baby.

Last night Tom kissed my stomach, and together we said good-bye to our child, a child we saw only on a screen. I am blessed that I first saw our baby when her heart was still beating; Tom saw her only still. But we knew this baby. We wanted her, and now she is gone. So we said good-bye before they took her away.

Alternately I feel numbness, then deep, searing pain. I sometimes have a frightening, reckless feeling that nothing matters.

I feel anger at God, then indifference toward Him, and then yearning for Him. I wonder if He's turned His back on me, but then I'm gripped by the thought that He's waiting, arms outstretched, waiting for me to run to Him, to grow somehow from this pain.

I'm confused by the idea that suffering is not coincidental, that it has a purpose. Does that mean God sends it deliberately? Or does He change our suffering, which comes to us randomly, if only we offer it up to Him, allowing Him to transform the chafe and pain into an iridescent pearl?

> … when I stood forlorn,
> Knowing my heart's best treasure was no more;
> That neither present time, nor years unborn
> Could to my sight that heavenly face restore.
>
> —William Wordsworth, "Surprised by Joy"[15]

CRACKERS MAKE ME CRY
From Karen Murphy Corr

Yes, crackers make me cry. Not just any crackers, and not all the time. But it seems as if baby loss has made even my biggest pregnancy craving a bittersweet reminder of my stillborn baby boy.

While expecting George, I craved Wasa bread crackers—the original ones, whole wheat, plain. They were like magic. I munched on them constantly, loving their taste and their satisfying crunch. They were the first thing I reached for in the morning, my constant snack of choice, and my preferred nighttime nibble over anything else, including potato chips and chocolate, even Swiss milk chocolate.

My husband teased that my incessant munching and crunching made me sound like a demented rodent. He thought I'd get tired of the plain kind and brought home rye and multigrain. I ate those too, but they weren't as good as the plain whole wheat, not by a long shot.

I thought this baby, our fifth child, would be a true West Coast granola child. I envisioned him eating these crackers with me, spurning unhealthy snacks as he balanced whole-grain goodness with fresh, locally grown produce.

But he died during my labor, and I'm devastated by this loss. So now, thinking of this craving makes me sad and wistful. I haven't eaten those crackers since George was born silent. I don't know if I will someday again, but I do know that even thinking about eating them is making me cry.

Am I crackers? [16]

· · ·

But for sorrow there is no remedy provided by nature; it is often occasioned by accidents irreparable, and dwells upon objects that have lost or changed their existence; it requires what it cannot hope, that the laws of the universe should be repealed; that the dead should return, or the past should be recalled.

—Samuel Johnson[17]

Did You Know?

Mother's Day is one of the hardest days of the year for those of us who have miscarried or are struggling with infertility. A card, a sympathetic e-mail, a phone call from a friend who understands—having someone reach out means a lot to us "invisible" mothers. Don't be afraid to ask for acknowledgment and support from those you love.

I many times thought peace had come,
When peace was far away;
As wrecked men deem they sight the land
At centre of the sea,

And struggle slacker, but to prove,
As hopelessly as I,
How many the fictitious shores
Before the harbor lie.

—Emily Dickinson[18]

Notes From My Journal

Even in the midst of our misery, there are small moments that touch my core—slow-dancing with Tom on the back patio, listening to "Someone to Watch Over Me" on a cool, spring night. My husband is a gift. I am blessed by him.

Mother's Day was difficult. I have conceived children, but no one considers me a mother. It is not a day for those like me: near-mothers,… failed mothers.

It's been a month since we lost the baby. Time passes so strangely through grief. At times I can feel as if it happened last week. Other days I feel as if it's been months and months since I was pregnant.

I am dreading my dentist appointment. I don't want to walk in there and have to say, "Oh, by the way, I had a miscarriage. You can do those X-rays now." I shouldn't have to tell my dentist that my baby died.

But that's what happened: My baby died. Both of my babies died. And that's the reality, a reality about which I must inform even my dentist.

HOLY BEYOND

From a mother who experienced multiple miscarriages,
on blogging and keeping a journal

I wish to have a place to honor my children I cannot hold. So sweet, so dear, so worthy of His love. They are now part of the Church Triumphant. And I sense that these vulnerable little beings, who could not sustain life here on earth, are just so radiant, wise, joyous, and holy beyond anything I could even hope to be here on earth.[19]

. . .

Did You Know?

Journaling can be a helpful and healthy way to express our grief. The act of writing often brings about release and catharsis. A journal can be as simple as a spiral notebook. Or you might want to choose something special and lovely in memory of your baby.

Blogging can be done privately (blogs can be set up as "invitation only" sites and can be hidden from search engines) or as part of a blogging community of like-minded women. There can be great benefit in sharing thoughts, feelings, and questions with others who are going through the same thing.

Fill your paper with the breathings of your heart.

—William Wordsworth[20]

Little Sparrow

No one scorns the haiku for being shorter than *War and Peace*
Nor scolds the daffodil for being briefer than a redwood.
But this little life cut off so young
We mourn and cry "too soon too soon."

Surely the Author knows when to end each tale

And yet
Jesus wept.

So should we all
For in the beginning death was not

And though there is a plan perhaps for even this little sparrow's
    fall
Still we cry
For we know that a sparrow was meant to fly.

—Melanie Bettinelli[21]

For God alone my soul waits in silence,
    for my hope is from him.
He only is my rock and my salvation,
    my fortress; I shall not be shaken.

—Psalm 62:5–6

. . .

Notes From My Journal

There is no understanding of this loss until it is experienced. I remember the face of my friend Janet after her second miscarriage (before I had experienced this myself). I struggled to find soothing words but probably said all the things people say that are so wrong: "You're young," "You'll have another," "It's nature's way, a blessing, really," "It happens to so many women."

And on her face was this infinitely sad, faraway look. I knew I wasn't reaching her. Nothing I said touched even the fringe of her sadness. She was deeply distressed, I knew that. But there was nothing I could do. I knew that too.

> We are not provided with wisdom, we must discover it for our-
> selves, after a journey through the wilderness which no one
> else can take for us, an effort which no one can spare us, for

our wisdom is the point of view from which we come at last to
regard the world.

—Marcel Proust, *Remembrance of Things Past*[22]

Answer me, O LORD, for your merciful love is good;
    according to your abundant compassion, turn to me.
Hide not your face from your servant;
    for I am in distress, make haste to answer me.

—Psalm 69:16–17

I Could Not Wake You

I dreamed you whole.
I carried you three months.

September October November

I could not wake you
my boy of perfection.
You did not die, only moved
from my belly to my back,

December January February

as heavy as a hood

of draped and folded sleep.

March April in May

The year
turns over.
Milkweed fusses
in waxy clumps.

June July August

Still you lie;
I, still, am waked.

—Sara Lewis Holmes[23]

You use the simple, obvious, yet now so rare, word *sad*. Neither
more nor less nor other than sad. It suggests a clean wound....
And I am sure it is never sadness—a proper, straight natural
response to loss—that does people harm, but all the other
things, all the resentment, dismay, doubt and self-pity with wh.
it is usually complicated.

—C.S. Lewis[24]

FATHERS ACHE TOO
From a father of two

The half truth that we are never told but somehow pick up on is that miscarriage is not a man's issue. The truth in there is that men and women suffer the loss of a child in different ways. The falsehood is that men are removed from suffering.

I was lousy when it came to responding to miscarriage in the moment. I was young, unmarried, and in no way ready to be a father. When I got the news of the miscarriage, I thought that I was off the hook, a free man. Now, a decade later, I wonder about the two little ones who daily are more and more conspicuous by their absence. I have a niece about the age my children would have been. When I see her I cannot help but want to see them—to watch them run around the corner, laughing and chasing their cousin. I think, though I am not sure why, that these two little ones were girls. My girls.

Though I am ashamed to say it, I was not at their mother's side at the moment of the miscarriage. There are so many reasons why, none of them good. My hope is that the mercy of God is a deep mercy and that these two young souls are in heaven now. If so, my one consolation is that in the perfection of heaven they have managed to forgive me, even if I struggle still with forgiving myself.

Healing is a much slower process than I thought it would be. Once people are loved, they are missed. The wound left behind is never fully healed. We never fall completely out of love with anyone. When we love, we give of ourselves sacrificially; what is given can be responded to in kind but never returned.

Though it may sound strange to say so, my love for my children increases with time, even though I have never held them in my arms. In moments when the emotion is overwhelming or so surprising that it leaves me breathless, I try to consider the alternative, that of having forgotten them entirely—an unconscionable possibility. Instead, I realize that my identity is as a father—that is for all time. Knowing this helps me try to live a life of integrity, one that would make my girls proud of their dad.

If any blessing has come as a result of all this, it is the intense desire to see my children. We Christians believe in the resurrection of the dead and the life of the world to come. I hope that if I live my life as well as I can and come to know Him more each day in prayer, Our Lord may place me under His mercy and, after the resurrection of the dead, I will be able to embrace my children for the first time and forever.

How I miss them.[25]

Be strong and let your heart take courage,
  all you who wait for the LORD.

—Psalm 31:24

Pair of Wings

Mommy and Daddy, you are in such pain,
but I can still see you, and you'll see me again.
My body was weak, but now my heart can sing,
for Jesus, He gave me this pair of wings....
We will never know the reasons, we'll never know the time.
We will never answer questions so heavy on our minds.
We might pray to see Jesus and demand the whys and hows ...
  Don't cry, Mommy, I can see Him now.
. . .
Dry your eyes, Daddy, I'm right here by your side.
Jesus will carry you when you feel your strength subside.
I'll be flying in heaven, don't worry about a thing.
I'll be waiting for you with my pair of wings

—Anthony Beardslee[26]

Silent Grief
From a single mother

I was in my early thirties and engaged to be married when I got pregnant. My fiancé was supportive; he suggested we move the wedding date up. We told everyone that the new date worked better with his schedule. (He was working on his master's degree.) Only three people knew about the pregnancy. I was afraid but happy. I remember walking around the office, feeling so special.

I was less than three months along when I miscarried. At the hospital the woman who performed my ultrasound broke the news. I couldn't believe it.

I missed work the next day—said I was having "female problems," and they asked no more questions. I was drained physically and emotionally, and I was so torn. I was relieved in a way—now no one had to know about our "mistake." I wasn't proud of what we'd done.

But now the baby was gone, and I felt empty, as if a huge hole had been left behind. I didn't feel special anymore, just very alone.

The hardest part was not being able to talk to anyone. I was a good girl, and I was afraid people would be shocked. I'm shocked! When people talk about miscarriages, I still do not feel able to join in the conversation.

I do have one child now; he's sixteen. I recently told him that I lost a baby many years ago. It meant a lot to him to know. He doesn't like being an only child, so I thought it would help him to know that someday, in heaven, he would meet his sibling, who I believe is a girl. I named her Erin, and I say good night to her every evening in my prayers.

So I tell myself the miscarriage was probably a good thing, that the baby wasn't forming correctly. But it still hurts. And I miss my baby. And I too look forward to seeing her someday in heaven.[27]

· · ·

Did You Know?

You need never feel alone, no matter what your circumstances. Jesus is waiting to hold and heal you in so many ways. Perhaps you have no friends who can relate or understand. Even so—even if you fear she won't "get it"—consider confiding in a friend. Risk talking about it.

Perhaps, like this silent mourner, you were single when you lost your baby. That's no reason to suffer alone. Try talking to your priest or someone you trust. Secrets can become heavy burdens.

There are support groups too, which can be lifesavers. Morning Light

Ministry offers telephone support at no cost. Share Pregnancy and Infant Loss Support, Inc., offers a 24/7 phone line and an online chat room. The Apostolate of Hannah's Tears offers a list of Catholic bloggers as a possible starting point for connecting with others. See the resources section for more details.

> For I know the plans I have for you, says the LORD, plans for welfare and not for evil, to give you a future and a hope. Then you will call upon me and come and pray to me, and I will hear you. You will seek me and find me; when you seek me with all your heart, I will be found by you, says the LORD.
>
> —Jeremiah 29:11–14

Notes From My Journal

My grandmother said something about my carrying "a few more pounds" than when she'd last seen me. "It looks good on you," she said breezily. I was devastated.

To her this extra weight is a simple shift in my appearance. To me it is a daily, painful reminder that I've been pregnant twice in the last year. And yet I do not have a child.

I am a different person in grief. Maybe everyone is. I wander around in a daze, as if I'm outside myself. I thrash in the rapids of the distress, and I don't know how to come up for air. How irrational and unsettling my feelings can be.

I wish I could explain to my friends how this feels. My miscarriages (it seems like such an innocent word, *miscarriage*…like *appendectomy*), my losses, the deaths of my babies, have been the most profound experiences of grief in my life. I have never felt anything like this before. I know myself as "normal," and I know myself in grief…and I cannot really say that I am the same person.

> When I no more can stir my soul to move,
> And life is but the ashes of a fire;
> When I can but remember that my heart
> Once used to live and love, long and aspire—
> Oh, be thou then the first, the one thou art;
> Be thou the calling, before all answering love,
> And in me wake hope, fear, boundless desire.
>
> —George MacDonald, *Diary of an Old Soul*[28]

Invisible Families

Many of us unconsciously think of "good Catholic families" as large families. But good Catholic families come in all sizes. When the number of children is "only" one or two children (or none at all, in the case of infertility), it might be the visible sign of parents who have suffered.

I do have a large family, but mine isn't visible to the world. As Tom and I suffered through our miscarriages, we gained powerful prayer warriors in heaven, but since they can't be seen they sometimes don't seem to "count." And that sometimes hurts. Questions such as "Did you want more?" or "Only three kids?" weren't meant to wound, but depending on the day or my mood or how recently I'd experienced a loss, they could be devastating.

Several years ago I met a friend's mother. She asked about children, and I proudly shared my daughters' (two of them, at the time) names and ages. She smiled politely. But when another guest mentioned her five kids, my friend's mother lit up. "That's wonderful!" she gushed. "So few people have that many these days!"

I'd lost a baby just two weeks prior. I wanted to shout, "I have more in heaven—doesn't that count?"

This woman didn't intend them to, but her words stung as sharply as if she'd slapped me. Had she known my situation, she would never have said what she did. She just didn't know. And of course, I remained silent.

Just as you want friends and family to be patient with you as you grieve, try to be patient with others who can't see or don't know about your beloved but invisible family. They don't mean to hurt you.

Sometimes it's appropriate to mention the babies you've lost. It's a judgment call, depending on the circumstances, but I've had such conversations go from awkward to amazing. Your babies in heaven might be just the people to awaken a new sensitivity in someone who has spoken without thinking.

· · ·

Notes From My Journal

I got a note from L in the mail and thought, "How sweet of her to send a sympathy card." I opened it and found an invitation to a baby shower. It felt like a slap. It's awful that I felt that way, but it's the truth. I don't blame L—this is not her fault. I just felt so sad. And sad that my grief and my loss are mostly invisible to the world.

To many, miscarriages are just things that happen in other families, so they are soon dismissed. Life goes on. It goes on for me too, yes—but I haven't forgotten my babies.

"The Musee des Beaux Arts," a poem by W.H. Auden, speaks to me about this idea of suffering and of the way we feel it so acutely as the world turns blithely on. Auden refers to the mundane things that occur—a window is opened, a neighbor goes out for a stroll—while we are still plunged in grief. Such a surreal juxtaposition. How can anyone care about the weather or a walk when we feel the world has ended?

For Birth or for Death?
From Margaret

I have just come from the follow-up ultrasound, where I learned that we have indeed lost our baby. December is becoming a tricky season for me to navigate: three pregnancies, three Advents, three miscarriages in a row. I am reminded of the poem "The Journey of the Magi" by T.S. Eliot, in which he asks, "Were we led all that way for birth or death?"[29]

This life is a mystery, that's for sure.

I am trying not to think too hard. The danger in times of deep sorrow—at least, for one who, like me, is prone to some depression—is to overanalyze and to doubt. God in His goodness sends us joy and suffering. The joy part is easy to welcome, but the suffering? Bah, humbug. I am dying to myself in ways I never asked for, yet I trust—I must trust—that it is for a greater good than any I may know in this lifetime.[30]

· · ·

Father,
I abandon myself into Your hands.
Do with me what You will.
Whatever You may do,

I thank You.
I am ready for all,
I accept all.
Let only Your will be done in me
and in all Your creatures.
I wish no more than this, O Lord.
Into Your hands
I commend my soul.
I offer it to You
with all the love of my heart.
For I love You, Lord,
and so need to give myself,
to surrender myself into Your hands
without reserve
and with boundless confidence.
For You are my Father.

—Fr. Charles de Foucauld[31]

How Long, Lord?
From B.

I've sat down a few times to try to write about my experience in losing our baby. I didn't expect this, but I don't think I can do it. It's still too painful, and it feels too soon to be able to share with anyone. Maybe that's my contribution—two years and one son later, I still grieve for the child we lost.[32]

. . .

Notes From My Journal

When I held a friend's new baby:

She's perfect. I couldn't help but think about what my babies would have looked like, and I wondered why some babies grow to perfection and others' hearts stop beating after nine weeks.

….It's been three months since my second miscarriage. We recently ran into an acquaintance who casually asked, "How's the baby?"

"I, uh—we lost the baby," I said, desperately holding back the tears that welled up.

It suddenly felt as if it had happened yesterday. The pain of having to voice it was on me like an attack. Tom said his response was to protect me: He wanted to cover me, shield me, deflect the incoming missile.

If a mother is mourning not for what she has lost but for what her dead child has lost, it is a comfort to believe that the child has not lost the end for which it was created. And it is a comfort to believe that she herself, in losing her chief or only natural happiness, has not lost a greater thing, that she may still hope to 'glorify God and enjoy Him forever.' A comfort to the God-aimed, eternal spirit within her. But not to her motherhood. The specifically maternal happiness must be written off. Never, in any place or time, will she have her son on her knees, or bathe him, or tell him a story, or plan for his future, or see her grandchild.

—C.S. Lewis, *A Grief Observed*[33]

ETERNAL GIFTS
From Ellen Gable Hrkach

I always wanted to be the mother of many. In high school, while friends were deciding what to do with their lives, my ambition was old-fashioned: marriage and motherhood. When I first met my husband, I shared with him my dream of a large family.

We have been blessed with eleven pregnancies, but not all have resulted in the birth of a child. We have five living sons and seven souls (including twins) in heaven. It was at times a very difficult journey.

In the aftermath of my third loss, I became extremely depressed. I forgot about my prayer life and sometimes neglected my two young sons. I cried when I saw pregnant women and mothers with newborns. I was angry at people who chose sterilization and threw away God's gift of fertility.

My husband, James, was sensitive and understanding, but he eventually lost patience. One night after the boys were in bed, he said, "Ellie, you need to focus on God, not on yourself. We need to start praying more." He reminded me that being open to God's will meant being open not only to having a large family but also to having a small family, if that was what God had planned. I realized that in my quest to have many children, I may have lost sight of what God wanted for me.

Through prayer and Scripture, I came to an acceptance of God's will for us. I now know a tiny portion of what Mary must have felt—carrying Jesus for nine months, nurturing and loving him for thirty-three years, only to have Him suffer and die in front of her. She accepted all this without question or doubt. Any suffering I have experienced has caused me to feel closer to Christ.

When I think of the seven babies we've lost, there is sadness that I never got to hold them. But each one was prayed for and loved from the moment of conception. Parental love drives us to guide our children to heaven. When we lose a baby through miscarriage, we have accomplished our goal: Our children are there. My seven children are great blessings, eternal gifts from a merciful God. [34]

• • •

Did You Know?

We all grieve in our own ways and on our own time lines but, if after what feels like a reasonable time for you, you find that you're not functioning well or fear that you've moved into a state of prolonged depression, don't hesitate to seek professional help. It is not weak or shameful to turn to counseling; rather it takes strength to recognize the need to reach out to those who know more about grief and suffering than we do. Talk to your priest or a counselor for recommendations.

Sometime after I'd experienced a couple of miscarriages, I heard that a colleague of my husband had just experienced a loss too. I barely knew Lori, but I felt compelled to send her a note of sympathy. We connected without hesitation, and neither of us felt awkward about sharing our personal and painful stories.

We discovered the kinship—knowing nods, embraces, talks, and understanding—of the sorrowful sisterhood of women who have lost children.

Have You Given Your Baby a Name?

Your baby had a life while she was in your womb. She died, but she possesses an eternal soul. Our precious children deserve to have names.

Names are powerful. They identify us, shape us, and connect us to one another. In Scripture, names often define missions. A name change indicates a new role and purpose. So Abram becomes Abraham, Sarai becomes Sarah, and Jacob is transformed into Israel. Simon becomes the rock, and Saul is shattered, resurrected as Paul. One name is the mission: Jesus means, and is, our Savior.

Names have meaning.

> But now thus says the LORD, he who created you, O Jacob,
>> he who formed you, O Israel:
> "Fear not, for I have redeemed you;
>> I have called you by name, you are mine."
>
> —Isaiah 43:1

Please don't feel guilty if you haven't named your baby. Perhaps you hadn't gotten beyond the stage of referring to your child only as "the baby." Perhaps you hadn't even thought of giving the baby a name, and that's understandable.

You may not know whether your baby was a boy or a girl, but don't worry about that either. Jesus knows. If you have a gut feeling about it, listen to that. If not, you might want to choose a name that works for either a boy or a girl. Some people choose first and middle names that cover both—for example, "Joseph Mary" or "Anna Simeon."

A name affirms the uniqueness and dignity of the child you lost. It is a small but very real gift you can give to the baby you were not able to see or embrace.

• • •

Did You Know?

The Church of the Holy Innocents in New York City houses a shrine to commemorate children who have died before birth. Its website tells us:

> Often children who have died before birth have no grave or headstone, and sometimes not even a name. At the Church of the Holy Innocents, we invite you to name your child(ren) and to have the opportunity to have your baby's name inscribed in our "BOOK OF LIFE." Here, a candle is always lit in their memory. All day long people stop to pray. On the first Monday

of every month, our 12:15 PM Mass is celebrated in honor of these children and for the comfort of their families. *We pray that you will find peace in knowing that your child(ren) will be remembered at the Shrine and honored by all who pray here.*[35]

Visit www.innocents.com and click on "Shrine of the Unborn" to enter your child's name in the "Book of Life" and to request a certificate in honor of your child.

For you formed my inward parts,
    you knitted me together in my mother's womb.
I praise you, for I am wondrously made.
    Wonderful are your works!
You know me right well;
    my frame was not hidden from you,
when I was being made in secret,
    intricately wrought in the depths of the earth.
Your eyes beheld my unformed substance;
    in your book were written, every one of them,
the days that were formed for me,
    when as yet there was none of them.

—Psalm 139:13–16

Notes From My Journal

I attended a baptism today, and I felt like a defective vessel in a sea of fertility.

> Hear my prayer, O LORD;
> > let my cry come to you!
> Do not hide your face from me
> > in the day of my distress!
> Incline your ear to me;
> > answer me speedily in the day when I call!

> For my days pass away like smoke,
> > and my bones burn like a furnace.
> My heart is struck down like grass, and withered;
> > I forget to eat my bread.
> Because of my loud groaning
> > my bones cling to my flesh.
> …
> I lie awake,
> > I am like a lonely bird on the housetop.

> —Psalm 102:1–5, 7

ADJUSTMENTS

From Janet Brungardt

I have been trying to adjust to the fact that I am not pregnant anymore. While pregnancy has its unpleasant parts (morning sickness, back pain, and so on), it is still such a joyful time, full of anticipation and dreams. What will the baby look like? How will he fit into the family? I look forward to the joys of baptism, how the other kids will dote on her, plans for room arrangements, and a thousand other things.

Then there are the things I do for my little baby in the womb: cut back on caffeine, avoid alcohol and most over-the-counter drugs, watch what I eat, avoid hot baths. Now, every time I have a little caffeine or take something for a headache, I'm reminded that I'm no longer pregnant. Last night I sank into a hot tub. I turned on the jets and mourned the fact that I could do that…because I am no longer pregnant.

Sometimes I am surprised when I realize that I feel lonely, even in the midst of my children. I miss my little baby, and I miss that bonding I always feel in pregnancy. I had started praying for her even before I knew that I was pregnant. I prayed for her and bonded with her even before conception. Then gradually I began to notice the changes in my body because of her. Life within me. And I rejoiced in her.[36]

She longed greatly to go back to those dear merry days when life was seen through a rosy mist of hope and illusion, and possessed an indefinable something that had passed away forever. Where was it now—the glory and the dream?

—L.M. Montgomery, *Anne of the Island*[37]

. . .

Did You Know?

Our Blessed Mother knows what we are feeling. Consider all that Mary endured. She was given the singular privilege of carrying Our Lord in her womb, but she also had to watch Him suffer and die. She said yes— she gave her *fiat*—every time.

Our Lady of Sorrows is waiting to pray for us. Ask for her intercession.

Ever-patient in her yearning
Though her tear-filled eyes were burning,
Mary gazed upon her Son.
Who, that sorrow contemplating,
On that passion meditating,
Would not share the Virgin's grief?

—From the *Stabat Mater*[38]

Mother! Call her with a loud voice. She is listening to you; she sees you in danger, perhaps, and she—your holy mother Mary—offers you, along with the grace of her son, the refuge of her arms, the tenderness of her embrace...and you will find yourself with added strength for the new battle.

—St. Josemaría Escrivá, *The Way*[39]

Notes From My Journal

An anxiety dream: I am surrounded by terrifying people, feeling I've been pressed into some corner of hell, when suddenly it strikes me that my protection, the only thing I've got, is this: "Lord Jesus Christ, Son of God, have mercy on me, a sinner." I repeat the Jesus Prayer, over and over, and I suddenly know these specters can't touch me, can't hurt me. They back away, and I feel the power of the prayer—His power against evil. It is the one thing that I can turn to and hold on to. My only power is recognizing that I have none and then calling on His power to help me.

I can do all things in him [Christ] who strengthens me.

—Philippians 4:13

Too Hard on Ourselves

A friend told me about her two miscarriages from years before. Jolene said she had never forgiven herself for the way she had handled them. Confused, I asked what she meant.

She explained that in the midst of the pain, the bleeding, and the confusion of one miscarriage, she could only conclude that her baby must have been flushed away with everything else. Another miscarriage, sixteen weeks into her pregnancy, required surgery. The doctor and the hospital staff simply explained to her what would happen and then proceeded. It was only when another friend talked about burial after a miscarriage that Jolene realized she had never been given that option. Now she feared she would end up in hell because she had not given her baby a proper burial and the respect and dignity due every human life.

My heart broke for Jolene. She had spent years feeling guilty for no reason. Our merciful Lord would never condemn a heartbroken mother to hell for something that is not a sin—something that she didn't know, couldn't help, and couldn't have changed at the time. Jolene had been dwelling on rules she thought she'd broken.

A healing Mass and talking with a priest helped her to realize that she need not fear God or continue to feel guilty. She was finally able to begin to truly recover from her losses.

. . .

Did You Know?

If your miscarriage happened in a way that prevented you from recovering or burying your baby's remains, please do not despair. You did your best. Your baby knows it, and so does our Lord.

With each of my losses I needed a D&C, as my body never properly labored. I was not a Catholic when I had my first two miscarriages and, admittedly, I did not give much thought to what happened to my babies' remains. The doctors explained things matter-of-factly. Beyond that, no one addressed the issue or seemed concerned.

Following my first loss as a Catholic, I panicked. I talked to my priest because, like my friend Jolene, I had a shattering fear that I had not done my babies justice. My spiritual director was on the ethics board of our local hospital, and he assured me that the facility was doing everything right. Babies lost through miscarriage were not treated as "waste"—remains were buried respectfully and services were offered several times a year for bereaved parents.

Some hospitals are immensely sensitive to our circumstances, offering a wide range of information and options, burial for miscarried children, annual memorial services, and connections with funeral homes. Others are not as informed or helpful. If your doctor or hospital did not offer you a full range of choices and you were unaware that anything was available, it's not your fault. In a time of fear, confusion, and grief, bereaved mothers and fathers shouldn't have to launch an investigation. As Jolene said to me, "My baby had died! That was all I could think about!"

Remind yourself that you did what you knew how to do at the time. If you feel the need to forgive yourself, do so—it will help you to move on in the grief process. Talk to your priest, and remember that God doesn't blame you for things you could not control. You can also inquire about the policies of your hospital and, for future reference, find out exactly how miscarriages are handled.

Trust the mercy of the God who loves you.

> For the desire of your heart is itself your prayer. And if the desire is constant, so is your prayer.
>
> —St. Augustine[40]

Notes From My Journal

Pregnant. After two miscarriages, I'm trying not to dwell on the fear, but I have to admit that the time line that creeps into my brain has more to do with when I'll lose a baby than when I'll have one. This is so hard.

> Let nothing trouble you, let nothing frighten you. All things are passing; God never changes. Patience obtains all things. He who possesses God lacks nothing: God alone suffices.
>
> —St. Teresa of Avila, "Bookmark" [41]

CRICKET IN A CUP

A quintessential summer evening, long ago. Every window in our tiny house was open, and soothing sounds wafted in: laughter from Elly, our six-year-old neighbor, playing with her big brothers; the chirping of crickets; the hypnotic whoosh-whoosh of the sprinkler in the backyard. It was the kind of evening that makes you happy just to breathe.

I, though breathing, was not happy. I was puzzling over our recent miscarriages and mulling over my new Christian faith. I had grown up without formal religion, embraced atheism, and for a number of years shunned all things traditional, including marriage and children. I'd barreled down a path of self-destruction, but God's plans got in my way, and He turned my life around.

After my conversion I assumed my dramatic about-face would yield sterling results. Life would be easier now, wouldn't it? Maybe even inch toward perfection? Yet here I was, a married Christian desperately longing for a baby, and what was my reward? Our first two attempts to start a family had ended in loss.

The chirping of the crickets grew a bit louder.

"How long are you going to be?" my husband called up the stairs.

"Just a couple minutes," I called back, opening my journal. "I'll be down when you start grilling."

The crickets chirped again. It sounded as if one was nearby. I turned back to my notebook. "Why do we have to endure these losses," I wrote, "when our intentions are finally in the right place?"

Chirp…chirp. I was getting irritated but continued scribbling. "God's plan is so obscure to me now. If there's a reason for losing our babies, I wish He would make it clear." *Chirp…chirp. CHIRP.*

Irked, I slapped the journal down and left the room. I returned with a paper cup and a firm resolve to pack up and relocate the cricket. Although I had no compunction about killing cockroaches, squashing spiders, or swatting flies, I didn't have the heart to dispatch a cricket. Perhaps I was still holding to a superstition from my pre-Christian days, a vague sense that cricket killing was bad karma. I felt compelled to catch crickets rather than stomp on them.

At the next chirp I located the offender and captured him. I headed downstairs and out the front door and released him in the yard, where he hopped off into the cool, green grass.

I sighed, thinking, "Well, at least he's happy again." As I walked back in the house, I was struck by a thought.

"What is it?" asked my husband, who met me in the kitchen. "You look confused or something."

"I'm the cricket," I said, eyes wide. Tom looked puzzled, possibly worried that I was flashing back to when I believed in reincarnation.

"Don't you see?" I repeated. "I'm the cricket! We're the crickets!" He shook his head.

"The cricket had to go outside, right? So I caught him in a cup and carried him out."

My husband, ever supportive but uncomprehending, nodded. "Oka-a-a-y," he said. "Go on."

"I knew I was doing a good thing for the cricket, that he'd be better off, but he didn't know that. While he was in the cup, all he knew was that he was trapped. He didn't understand."

"Exasperating things, crickets. They don't understand anything," my husband said, smiling.

I slapped his arm. "Listen!" I said. "When he was finally back outside, he knew he was home. But before that, he couldn't possibly know that the cup was a good thing, that it was helping him. Don't you see?"

My husband smiled and nodded. "We're the crickets."

"Yes. We're in the scary, awful dark, and we don't understand about our babies. But when God is finished carrying us through all this, maybe we'll be able to see what the cup was. Then we'll know."

"Then we'll know," he said. He smiled and kissed me with all the affection I would expect from the father of my children. He went to start the hamburgers.

And in the sublime, soft light of that summer evening, I whispered a prayer of thanksgiving for a simple but seismic shift. God was cupping us in His hands. He always would. I knew that I was learning to live in His time, to accept being cradled for a while in darkness, if that was what His merciful love deemed necessary. And for the first time since the last miscarriage, I was happy just to breathe.

> May you be strengthened with all power, according to his glorious might, for all endurance and patience with joy, giving thanks to the Father, who has qualified us to share in the inheritance of the saints in light.
>
> —Colossians 1:11–12

A Grief Too Familiar

From Margaret

I don't know why, and I have no words of wisdom. I am numb and will pass through at least seven more stages of numbness before the grief sets in. I know these feelings very well by now; they are an unwelcome guest, and yet not really, because they represent my cross, and I must embrace it.[42]

. . .

Did You Know?

There are many local and national support organizations that can help you through both the immediate experience and the aftermath of a miscarriage. An excellent organization is the Elizabeth Ministry, as is Share Pregnancy and Infant Loss Support. Each offers a wide range of resources, from concrete help with the painful details of miscarrying at home to saving your baby's remains and planning a respectful burial. Books, pamphlets, and memorial items are also available. (See the resources section for more details.)

O LORD, you are our Father;
　　we are the clay, and you are our potter;
　　we are all the work of your hand.

—Isaiah 64:8

Notes From My Journal

When the doctor began the ultrasound, I simply began to pray. Our Father…I don't see a heartbeat…who art in heaven…he's measuring…there's no heartbeat…he wants to see how big the baby was before he died…Hail Mary, full of grace…Please, God, no….

My third miscarriage.

I feel, in many ways, stronger than I was through the last ones—my faith is stronger, and that helps me. But still…I feel incalculably sad. I wanted this baby so much. All signs seemed to point to the Lord's wanting us to have this baby too.

I have to admit to repeating that old line of St. Teresa of Avila, that if this is how He treats His friends, then it is not surprising that He has so few of them.

Fiat

For James Matthias Edmisten

You said that we would have a child.
So I welcomed new life
and smiled with each wave and sea
of morning sickness,
caught up in this miracle-to-be.
"For You, Lord," I said,
and offered each tiny suffering
as a gift to Thee,
incomparable to the gift of life
You would give to me.
And so I reeled, stunned and shaken,
at my baby's death.
I was forsaken.
Anger rose and built a case
against misinterpreted signs of Grace.
I was so wrong—
"Here is a child," You said,
or so I thought.
But my arms are empty, bereft.

There is nothing left of my trust
when I listen for Your Voice.
How can I trust when I was so wrong?
How will I again be strong?
I quiet myself and turn to You,
O Ancient Beauty ever new.
I ask You, my truest and deepest Love,
for an answer, some comfort,
a sign from above.
There is silence, and my tears…
tears of a mother's grieving love.
Then, in Your Kindness,
Your encompassing Love,
You embrace me and speak:
The words from above
flow through an earthen vessel.
A man of God who listens to me
and tells me I can—
I must—dare trust,
for all is as it should be.
The mystery that is my child

is in Your Hands,
Your Sacred Heart.
The part I play is to surrender and be free.
When next I quiet myself to pray,
"My grace is sufficient for you," You say,
"for My power is made perfect in weakness."
The words play again and again in my mind,
like a record left to skip…
they rip into the core of my grief
and leave me no choice but to drop to my knees
and offer You my child.
Oh, heal my heart, Lord, bitter and spent,
Be perfect in my weakness,
my Pearl of great price.
Though I offer it, Lord, imperfectly and poorly,
my life is Yours.
Let Your grace suffice.

The Power of One Small Life
From Mary DeTurris Poust

August 6. It was twelve years ago today that I learned that the baby I was carrying, my second baby, had died eleven weeks into my pregnancy.

With a mother's intuition, I had known something was wrong the day Dennis and I—with our young son Noah in tow—went to the midwife for my regular checkup. I didn't even take our little tape recorder to capture the sound of the baby's heartbeat, I was so convinced that I would hear only silence. (I went back for the recorder only after Dennis insisted.) But somehow I knew. Because when you are a mother, sometimes you just know things about your children, even when there is no logical reason you should, even when they are still growing inside you.

When we went for an ultrasound to confirm the miscarriage, we saw the perfect form of our baby up on the screen. Dennis looked so happy, thinking everything was OK after all, but I pointed out that the heart was still. No blinking blip. No more life.

With that same mother's intuition, no matter how busy or stressed I am, no matter how many other things I seem to forget as I drive my other three children to and fro, I never forget this anniversary. It is imprinted on my heart. As the date nears, I feel a stillness settling in, a quiet place amid the chaos reserved just for this baby, the one I never got to hold, the one I call Grace.

When I last wrote about this day, I talked about how Grace had shaped our family by her absence rather than her presence. I am very much aware that life would be very different had she lived. She managed to leave her mark on us, even without taking a breath. She lingers here, not only in my heart but around the edges of our lives—especially the lives of our two girls who followed her. I know them because I did not know Grace. What a sorrowful and yet beautiful impact she had on us.

So thank you, baby, for all that you were and all that you have given us without ever setting foot on this earth. The power of one small life.[43]

· · ·

If everything is lost, thanks be to God
If I must see it go, watch it go,
Watch it all fade away, die
Thanks be to God that He is all I have
And if I have Him not, I have nothing at all
Nothing at all, only a farewell to the wind
Farewell to the grey sky

Good-bye, God be with you evening October sky.
If all is lost, thanks be to God,
For He is He, and I, I am only I.

—Fr. Julian Stead[44]

Did You Know?

Helping our living children deal with a miscarriage can be an enormous challenge. When we're also grieving, it's hard to sort out what we need from what our children need. Reading about how others have handled it can help. See the resources section on page 125 for some titles.

Notes From My Journal

"I have to tell you about something," I said to my five-year-old. "You see…something happened, and the baby stopped growing. So…the baby has already gone to heaven to be with God."

She stared at me, utterly astonished. "You mean it *died?*"

"Yes, sweetie," I said. (Oh, Lord, help me.) "The baby died."

She dissolved, puddled into my arms, and we cried together.

Later, when I put her to bed, Emily suddenly sat up, cried again, and said, "There's something I forgot to do before the baby stopped growing! Oh, no! I forgot to put my hand on your tummy to feel the baby kick!"

I felt my heart crack. And I felt—what? Panic. I assured her that it was too early for her to have felt such a thing, and that it wasn't her fault, she didn't forget anything. But, oh, how will I deal with my own grief and fears and those of my children too? Can I do this? I was overwhelmed.

Later when I talked to Fr. Joe, he offered four little words that swiftly brought me peace: "The Lord will provide," he said. I felt as if I'd been handed a delicate gift wrapped in wisdom.

Simple. True. The Lord will provide. I stood firm again on my foundation.

What's Good These Days

Freshly cut irises in a vase on the dining-room table. Hearing "I'm so sorry." Our new kitten, Truman. A meal that a friend cooked and delivered, complete with chocolate cake. Tom's presence, support, love, and understanding. My daughters' beautiful faces, their laughter, their silliness, their incandescent love. Fr. Joe coming over for dinner and to pray with us. Letters, notes, phone calls from friends.

> Dead my old fine hopes
> and dry my dreaming,
> but still…
> iris, blue each spring.

—Shushiki[45]

What's Bad These Days

I lost my baby and I miss him.

Too much chocolate, too much sleep—too much numbing that doesn't really numb. And this drifting, uncertain feeling. Where do we go from here?

God instructs the heart not by ideas but by pains and contradictions.

—Fr. Jean Pierre de Caussade[46]

What Has Helped Me Through the Grief This Time

"The Lord will provide." Fr. Joe's simple exhortation offered me needed truth. No matter how sad or bad I feel, He will provide.

Reflecting on an Ascension homily: Trust in times of waiting. The apostles, between Ascension and Pentecost, had no idea what awaited them. We know that Pentecost was on the way, but they didn't know that. Bewildered, they saw Jesus leave them yet again. But they trusted and waited, and He sent the tremendous gift of His Spirit. Even when we are walking blindly, our trust must be complete.

Praying the Liturgy of the Hours and reading the book of Job: "Shall we receive good at the hand of God, and shall we not receive evil?" (Job 2:10).

My belief in redemptive suffering: The sacrifice of Christ was not for nothing. And as I offer my sufferings in prayer for the conversion of my husband, I know that I can willingly let go of my son to bring his father to Christ. But it is costing me—in grief, in struggle and in sadness, in releasing my version of what should be. Father, as always, Your will be done, not mine.

The prayer service for our sweet James Matthias.

> Down under the frozen crusts, at the roots of the trees, the
> secret of life was still safe, warm as the blood in one's heart; and
> the spring would come again! Oh, it would come again!
>
> —Willa Cather, *O Pioneers!*[47]

. . .

Did You Know?

Making a list of healing moments—gifts, sympathy cards, phone
calls, meaningful prayers, caring words, acts of kindness, shoulders to
cry on—can help you recall God in this time of grief. Try to keep an
ongoing list of people, events, and things for which you are grateful.
Refer to it when you're feeling especially sad.

Notes From My Journal

I've been trying to stay busy. My dear friend told me gently that she
thought, although activity is good, I've perhaps been busying myself
too much. The things I really need to make time for are prayer, silence,
relaxing, and healing. She's right. I've been so busy trying to feel "pro-
ductive." But no level of productivity can make up for the fact that I did
not produce a baby. I just need to feel that. And keep wading through it.

My girls (ages six and three now) and I always greet Jesus as we pass a Catholic Church. Today as we drove by Sacred Heart we called out, "Hi, Jesus! We love you!" as we always do. Then Lizzy said, "Wait…what was that?"

"What was what?" I asked.

"That whisper…it was Jesus. He said, 'I love you too.'"

Where, O Death, Is Your Victory?

When I first joined the ranks of Christianity, I naively assumed all my problems with death were over. When others spoke with sadness of someone dying, I thought, "But they've gone to heaven. Shouldn't we be cheering? They've made it! Do we believe this stuff or not?"

Of course, I was young and stupid. I hadn't experienced death much at all. I still had my parents and my grandparents. I grew up, for the most part, without funerals.

In college my boyfriend's brother died in a terrible car accident. Dave's was the first funeral I remember. Ironically or providentially, it was in the same town to which I'd later move and the same parish where I was eventually received into the Catholic Church. But what I remember most about the funeral is the crying—my tears and others'—over the waste of such a young life at the hands of a drunk driver. I felt dazed throughout the luncheon afterward. I didn't understand how we were supposed to eat, laugh, and chat as if we were mingling at a party. I just didn't know how to act. And I really didn't understand all that food.

Since that day I've had to say good-bye to all my beloved grandparents. My mother-in-law and father-in-law have passed away too. My husband and I saw old college friends lose their six-year-old daughter to a devastating blood disease. When another old friend was in a car accident, his ten-year-old daughter was critically injured and her best friend was killed. A friend from our parish lost his adult son suddenly due to an undiagnosed medical condition.

Of course, there have been other encounters with death. My miscarriages. People from church. The parents of our friends. Death is no longer a mysterious stranger, and my children have encountered it at a younger age than I did. And the lessons I've learned are these:

- While death may not be a mystery to a Christian, we are weak creatures who deal with it haltingly. No matter how glorious the new dwelling place of our friends and family, we miss them. It hurts. And we cry. Jesus wept too (see John 11:35), so we're in excellent company.
- No matter how young children are, they're deeply affected by loss, even if they do not know how to show it. And their feelings about grandparents dying and funeral attendance can get knotted up with their feelings about the hamster dying or the fact that they have brothers and sisters in heaven. And it's hard to sort out exactly what's making them cry, but one thing is certain: Sometimes they just need to be held. Just like me.

- And all that food that used to confound me? Now I know that food expresses love.

As Christians, we know that death does not have the final word for us. In spite of our sobs and our loneliness, our trials, fears, and pains, death's sting will not, in the end, win. Because Christ has conquered death. And so we can say:

> I will greatly rejoice in the LORD,
>   my soul shall exult in my God;
> for he has clothed me with the garments of salvation,
>   he has covered me with the robe of righteousness,
> as a bridegroom decks himself with a garland,
>   and as a bride adorns herself with her jewels.
>
> —Isaiah 61:10

Notes From My Journal

My fourth miscarriage…

Daily there are realizations that everything is different. I can take an aspirin, have a glass of wine, drown in coffee. Because there is no baby.

This is the hardest part about death: One day someone is part of every aspect of your life, and the next day she has vanished. All our plans for next spring, next summer, next year, are radically different. Because there is no baby.

There is no baby.

I don't know if there will ever be another baby. And that is hard too, to walk in the darkness, not knowing what the Lord's plan for us is. Knowing that, in being open to life, we may feel this same sorrow again.

How many D&Cs can one body take? How many miscarriages can my heart take?

I have dreams in which I've had a baby but I can't see her, hold her, or touch her. I call out for her, scream for someone to bring her to me, but no one will. I can't have her, and I awake feeling anguished.

> Each that we lose takes part of us;
> A crescent still abides,
> Which like the moon, some turbid night,
> Is summoned by the tides.
>
> —Emily Dickinson[48]

Divine Safeguards

From Abigail Benjamin

I'm profoundly grateful that I was a Catholic (instead of the happy, vaguely Christian woman I once was) before my miscarriage. The Catholic Church has clear rules that act as safeguards when we're in trouble. And when the nurse practitioner told me that my baby no longer had a heartbeat—the baby whose teeny fingertips I could now make out on the screen—I was in trouble.

I needed gentleness. I needed my husband and the anchor of a sacramental marriage. I needed the support of my beloved parish priest, who helped me discern the conception of this baby and then helped me plan the baby's funeral. I needed Catholic friends who treated this miscarriage as the loss of a real child.

At the same time, I needed some strict discipline because, the Sunday after my miscarriage, I couldn't face going to church.

My husband had spearheaded the effort to get two toddlers and me ready for Mass and to our bus stop on time. When the bus was late, I walked a few feet away from my family, ignored my good clothes, and lay down in the grass. "I cannot bear to go to church right now!" I said.

"Are you feeling bad?" my husband asked with some anxiety. "I can take the kids alone or go another time, if you don't feel well enough for Mass."

"No, I'm physically fine. It's a mental thing. I just cannot bear to go to Mass. Last week we were all there together. I rubbed my tummy and felt so happy. We got chocolate milkshakes afterward. I was excited that one day we'd be buying milkshakes for three kids."

"You can stay home," he said. "I'm sure it's all right."

"No." I wished I were Protestant again and could skip church whenever I wanted to.

But my "Sunday obligation" saved me. Because if I hadn't gone to Mass on that terrible Sunday when I was so mad at God, I don't know when I would have returned. It might have been only a week, but it probably would have been much, much longer.

My mother was once a Sunday-school administrator at our Protestant church. I remember her talking about a woman named Sandra who hadn't been in church in the two years since her father's death but was now planning to teach Sunday school. "Having her teach Sunday school will be such a beautiful way to get her back into the church," my mother said.

As Catholics we can't opt out while we manage our grief. We don't take a break and arrange our faces before we meet God. Each Sunday we're required to be in a pew at Mass. And that is not a pain-in-the-neck requirement. That is a grace. Because it is when we are bleeding and in pain, when we are angry and lost, when we most don't want to be in a church, that God has the most to say to us.

I was so mad—mad at pregnant mothers who blithely complained about "life with this baby" and who didn't realize that the gift of life can disappear in a second, mad and overwhelmed by the thought of seeing our church and its happy, stained-glass portraits of Mary cradling her newborn Jesus. But mostly I didn't want to go to Mass because I couldn't bear to have life go on as normal. I couldn't bear to have others forget my son.

I walked into the church feeling bitter and closed. "I'm here only because You are making me!" I thought. Then I found a figurine that Alex had left in our pew the week before. It was about four inches long—the same size as my dead son's body. I held it, cradled it tightly in my hand all during Mass.

The stained-glass window behind our regular pew was of our Blessed Mother holding Jesus—not as a newborn but after the crucifixion. I scooted into the blue shadow from that window. "Mary lost a son," I thought. "She knows how I feel."

I cried openly all through that Mass. I didn't get the sense then, squeezing my little doll and wishing that Francisco's body was back in my womb, that my being a Catholic mom made my burden easier. But now I do.

Catholicism has hard rules, but the Church is our mother. And when our way is blurred with tears, the Church makes sure our grief doesn't harden our hearts. Holy Mother Church can't prevent all of our pain, but she bandages our wounds and showers us with kisses.[49]

• • •

Consider the heroic faith of Mary in those dark moments on Good Friday. Gabriel originally told her that she would be the mother of Israel's Messiah, the mother of the One whose kingdom would have no end. Yet as John Paul II points out, at the foot of the cross Mary would be a witness, from a *human* perspective, to the complete negation of those words about Christ's everlasting kingship....

How great then must have been her trust as she entered what could be called a "spiritual crucifixion," letting go of her son and abandoning herself to God's care in this time of darkness.

—Edward Sri, *The New Rosary in Scripture*[50]

Behold, we know not anything;
I can but trust that good shall fall
At last—far off—at last, to all,
And every winter change to spring.

So runs my dream; but what am I?
An infant crying in the night;
An infant crying for the light,
And with no language but a cry.

—Alfred Lord Tennyson, *In Memoriam, A.H.H.* [51]

LIFE AND SANITY
From Karen Murphy Corr

I like the positive focus of my support group this month, because I've been feeling really rough the last few weeks. I'm just getting through moment to moment. Other mothers have been a tremendous support to me, and of course my husband.

But in our journey of grief some things stand out the most:

- A grandmother from our parish called me two days after George had died and suggested I change our voice mail, letting callers know there was no happy update on our babe's birth. This allowed my husband to not answer the phone, let people know we needed time, and got the word out that our boy had died. This friend offered to leave her name and number on the voice mail so she could coordinate things for us.

- Mothers from school made lunches for our boys, dropped off meals, and helped with transportation. Dear friends took the preschoolers for the first few days (and anytime we needed help with child care).

- My midwives loved my husband and me through the first few moments of saying good-bye to George. So kind and compassionate, especially their searching for sage tea to help me reduce my milk supply.

- Elders of the Squamish Nation blessed us with a blanket ceremony. I still feel wrapped in their care when I sit wrapped in our blanket.
- Letters arrived from the charities to which we'd asked people to donate in lieu of flowers. Beautiful letters came from the hospital foundation. Enough people donated to perinatal care that we will have a star on the wall of memory with George's name.
- I owe my life and my sanity to other baby-loss blogging mums, my bereaved friend Ellie, and Bernadette at Morning Light Ministries.[52]

· · ·

Notes From My Journal

After my fifth miscarriage…

When, on a day that already held the remembrance of a past grief for me, I had an ultrasound and found out my baby was dead, I was crushed. Bewildered, really, that the news came so cruelly on this particular date. "Why, Lord?" I implored. "Why on this day? I wanted this to be a day of life, not another day of death!"

Gently my Father spoke quietly in my heart. "This is not a day of death," I felt Him whisper to my aching soul, "but a day of life for your baby, because he is with Me, sharing eternal life, as are all your children. You hoped that today would conjure some kind of earthly redemption, but no earthly thing can redeem. I redeemed you when I died on the cross for you. Let go of your earthly despair. Be at peace."

I lift up my eyes to the hills.
From where does my help come?
My help comes from the LORD,
who made heaven and earth.

He will not let your foot be moved,
he who keeps you will not slumber.

—Psalm 121:1–3

The Beauty of Grief From a Distance
From Mary DeTurris Poust

Although I've written about grief and talked about grief, I am always awed by grief—by the way it can return in different forms on special dates and anniversaries, at the sound of a song or in the scent of a flower. In some ways this grief from a distance—not the anguished and desperate grief of the early days after a death but the aged and quiet grief over someone long gone—can be a beautiful thing. It's a way to revisit a life, to spend some time reliving moments shared, and to remember that we never really lose our connection. We are joined by our faith, in our prayers, in our hearts.

So today I pray for Grace, who will remain in my heart until I finally get to meet her.[53]

. . .

The Skin Horse had lived longer in the nursery than any of the others. He was so old that his brown coat was bald in patches and showed the seams underneath, and most of the hairs in his tail had been pulled out to string bead necklaces. He was wise, for he had seen a long succession of mechanical toys arrive to boast and swagger, and by-and-by break their mainsprings and pass away, and he knew that they were only toys, and would never turn into anything else. For nursery magic is very strange and wonderful, and only those playthings that are old and wise and experienced like the Skin Horse understand all about it.

"What is REAL?" asked the Rabbit one day, when they were lying side by side near the nursery fender, before Nana came to tidy the room. "Does it mean having things that buzz inside you and a stick-out handle?"

"Real isn't how you are made," said the Skin Horse. "It's a thing that happens to you. When a child loves you for a long, long time, not just to play with, but REALLY loves you, then you become Real."

"Does it hurt?" asked the Rabbit.

"Sometimes," said the Skin Horse, for he was always truthful. "When you are Real you don't mind being hurt."

"Does it happen all at once, like being wound up," he asked, "or bit by bit?"

"It doesn't happen all at once," said the Skin Horse. "You become. It takes a long time. That's why it doesn't happen often to people who break easily, or have sharp edges, or who have to be carefully kept. Generally, by the time you are Real, most of your hair has been loved off, and your eyes drop out and you get loose in the joints and very shabby. But these things don't matter at all, because once you are Real you can't be ugly, except to people who don't understand."

"I suppose *you* are real?" said the Rabbit. And then he wished he had not said it, for he thought the Skin Horse might be sensitive. But the Skin Horse only smiled.

"The Boy's Uncle made me Real," he said. "That was a great many years ago; but once you are Real you can't become unreal again. It lasts for always."

—Margery Williams, *The Velveteen Rabbit*[54]

My Broken Rosary

It was just before Thanksgiving, and I was at the doctor's office. The image on the ultrasound screen was not what it should have been.

"I'm concerned it may be ectopic," said my obstetrician, "but early ultrasound can fool us." He told me to come back in five days and did his best to assure me that all would be well.

I left feeling frightened and terribly sad. I was seven weeks along. We should have seen a heartbeat.

Five days later there was no sign of trouble in the fallopian tube, and the baby was indeed in the womb, but we still could not detect a heartbeat. My doctor wanted one more ultrasound in a few days—could we have miscalculated the date of conception, he wondered? Not likely, I said, for a couple who know the finer points of natural family planning. I feared the worst.

I reported the news to my closest friends with sadness. "No heartbeat," was all I could manage to say. They offered me prayers and shoulders to cry on.

One friend remained upbeat. "Hang on until the next ultrasound," she urged. "We have no idea what God has in store for your little one.

Pray to Our Lady of Guadalupe, the protector of the unborn." And so began the rosaries, asking for Our Lady's intercession.

A few days later I unexpectedly received a delicate rosary in the mail, a gift from a pro-life organization to which we'd donated. It bore the image of Our Lady of Guadalupe. My heart jumped, and I dared to hope this was a sign of an impending miracle.

The next day my four-year-old begged to hold the sparkling rosary on the drive to the home of a friend who would watch the kids while I went to my doctor's appointment. When we arrived at my friend's house, the rosary was in pieces. "I'm sorry, Mama," my little girl said with sad eyes. "It broke." Beads and links were scattered everywhere.

"It's OK," I told her. "Things break. You didn't mean to."

But inside I feared that my "sign" had broken too. I'd been trusting in my prayers to Our Lady of Guadalupe, and now my rosary, the unexpected gift that had prompted me to hope for a miracle, was in pieces.

Later, at the doctor's office, the final news came: no growth, no heartbeat. Blood tests later confirmed that the baby had died.

In my grief I forgot for a time about my broken rosary, but then a strange thing happened. Though I mourned our lost child, circumstances surrounding the miscarriage led to surprising resolution of a painful old emotional wound. What an amazing grace. I thanked God for what He had done through the short life and the death of my child.

It was then that I remembered the rosary. I pieced it back together and saw that I had nearly all of it. One decade lacked two beads, and my tinkering left the rosary crooked here and there, but it was repaired.

I was struck by the incongruity. This once perfect object was now bent and imperfect yet still beautiful. Like us, like our lives. Though we are made in the perfect image of God, we are bent with original sin; even after baptism we are crippled by sin's aftereffects. We stumble through life, tarnishing the perfect image while Our Lord repeatedly tinkers with us, repairs us, and heals us.

I'd imagined that the gift of the rosary meant that I would receive the gift of my baby. The healing I received instead was a great gift I could not have predicted. This unexpected rosary seemed to be a symbol of God's work in a broken part of my life.

Now, when I pray with my broken rosary, I think of my baby, and I know that my friend was right: We had no idea what God had in store for my little one. He is always, ineffably, making crooked ways straight.

· · ·

Notes From My Journal

As Christmas approached…

I was at Mass, praying in that way I have that gets a bit desperate: "What now, Lord? Where do we go next? Adoption? Or not? Do we stop now, with the children we have, or persevere? Do we try to have another child? What?"

Then I shut my mouth (always a good idea for me), and I tried to listen. I felt a lovely peace come over me, as if Jesus were wrapping his arms around me and saying, "Karen, would you just calm down? Relax, and enjoy my birthday. Take joy in your husband and your daughters. And we'll talk about all this later."

So that's what I did.

Thank you, Jesus.

Shut up he explained.

—Ring Lardner, *The Young Immigrants* [55]

Something to Do

A dear friend is in the midst of a miscarriage, and my heart is aching. Other friends have had losses recently too. I remember the pain of my own miscarriages and, although I firmly believe that Christ was with me through them all—He led me, sculpted me, and changed me—I also firmly believe we must grieve.

I know that my friends have an arduous path ahead of them. I want to do it for them, to take their grief away so they don't have to wade through it. I want to carry their crosses, save them from their pain.

But it doesn't work that way. I can't determine the pace of their healing. I am not at the center of their storms. I can merely stand by and offer help—try to pick up a few pieces, pat something back into place, offer food in the time of rebuilding.

That sounds feeble and doesn't seem like enough, yet it's all I can do. It's what I'm able to do. And it gives me *something* to do. Someone else has the job of genuinely taking on their burdens.

> Come to me, all who labor and are heavy laden, and I will give you rest. Take my yoke upon you, and learn from me; for I am gentle and lowly in heart, and you will find rest for your souls.

For my yoke is easy, and my burden is light.

—Matthew 11:28–30

Jesus Christ is the only one who can bring authentic peace and real understanding. Into His arms these women will fall and cry, as often as they need to. And I'll be there, doing what I can, with prayers, and plates of cookies, and tears of my own.

And one day, I pray, they will see His face in the face of their loss.

If I can stop one heart from breaking,
I shall not live in vain;
If I can ease one life the aching,
Or cool one pain,
Or help one fainting robin
Unto his nest again,
I shall not live in vain.

—Emily Dickinson[56]

. . .

Notes From My Journal
Still trying to decipher what to do next…

I was at a healing retreat, and in the confessional Fr. F. told me to simply consecrate my fertility to Jesus. "In about an hour," he said, "we will be at Holy Mass. At the moment of the Consecration, hand your fertility over to Jesus. Picture it as a precious gift you can hold in your hand. Place it gently on the paten with the bread that will become His body. Trust Him. Give it to Him. Completely. Then let it go. He'll make the rest clear."

Praying in Grief

Out of the depths I cry to you, O Lord!
   Lord, hear my voice!
Let your ears be attentive
   to the voice of my supplications!
. . .
I wait for the Lord, my soul waits,
   and in his word I hope;
my soul waits for the Lord
   more than watchmen for the morning,
   more than watchmen for the morning

O Israel, hope in the Lord!
   For with the Lord there is mercy,
   and with him is plenteous redemption.

—Psalm 130:1–2, 5–7

Sometimes it's hard for me to pray when I'm grieving. I don't know what to say, what to pray. I often don't even know how to move forward.

In such times I revisit a way of praying that I explored when I was first approaching Christianity. I prayed the Our Father just one word or phrase at a time, meditating on what the words said to me personally, in the moment. St. Thérèse described this method well:

> Sometimes when my mind is in such a great aridity that it is impossible to draw forth one single thought to unite me with God, I *very slowly* recite an "Our Father" and then the angelic salutation; then these prayers give me great delight; they nourish my soul much more than if I had recited them precipitately a hundred times.[57]

One slowly prayed Our Father can be worth hours of meditation for me. Think about it.

"Our Father": He is my loving Father. He knows exactly what I'm feeling.

"Who art in heaven": And my children are there with Him. He is my goal; heaven is my goal.

"Hallowed be Thy name": God is holy and wants me to be holy. Everything that He has allowed is for my good, even when I cannot begin to fathom why and even when it's painful.

"Thy kingdom come, Thy will be done": Isn't this the hardest thing? I want my Father's will to be done, but it hurts. Yet I must return to these words again and again. "Thy will be done."

> For this reason I bow my knees before the Father, from whom every family in heaven and on earth is named, that according to the riches of his glory he may grant you to be strengthened with might through his Spirit in the inner man, and that Christ may dwell in your hearts through faith; that you, being rooted and grounded in love, may have power to comprehend with all the saints what is the breadth and length and height and depth, and to know the love of Christ which surpasses knowledge, that you may be filled with all the fulness of God.
>
> —Ephesians 3:14–19

After All We've Been Through

It was November 2001. In the previous three weeks, we'd gotten an offer on our house (which had been on the market for seven months), swiftly packed everything, desperately hunted down an apartment, closed on the house, and moved. Right after moving day, all four of us came down with stomach flu. Then, just as we recovered from the stress of major life changes and a nasty virus, I noticed something. A test confirmed my suspicions.

I was pregnant. *Can I do this again*, I thought?

Emily and Lizzy were eight and five. I'd had five miscarriages, and the last two had been due to chromosome abnormalities that occur more frequently as women age. I'd be forty-two when this baby was born, if we made it past the first trimester.

I felt the familiar knot of dread in my stomach, and I was horribly confused about God's timing. After so many heartbreaks the desire for another baby had begun to wane. Just a few months earlier I'd surrendered to God.

"You win!" I'd conceded. "If we're not meant to have more children, I accept that."

I had settled into the routine of homeschooling my daughters. The pace felt right, our lives were pleasant and fun. "The Lord," I thought, "obviously knows what He's doing in limiting our family size." Exasperated surrender had evolved into serene acceptance.

So when I found out I was pregnant again, I was blindsided. Given my age and history, all I felt was intense fear.

I hated how consuming the feeling was. One morning I asked the Lord to take my fear and transform it. Almost immediately I was calmed. I could almost hear Him say (with a little "tsk-tsk" in His voice), "Don't you trust Me? After all we've been through together? Don't you know that whatever happens will be for your good and My glory?" Fear and stress seemed to slip away.

A few days later, however, my weakness returned. The "what ifs" began: "What if I'm too old? What if the baby is born sick? What if I can't do this? Or what if I lose this one too?" I had nightmares and felt restless all day.

I turned again to prayer, and abruptly a new thought occurred to me: "What if I have this baby for only a very short time, and I allow that time to be consumed by fear rather than love? How terrible would it be—for me and for this baby—if I lose it without ever having said, 'I love you'?" The possibility was sobering.

Fear has an insidious way of drawing me away from the Lord, placing me squarely in the grip of chaotic thoughts. But now, mercifully, I knew the truth. Whether the Lord allowed me to keep this baby for a few more minutes or days, a few weeks, an entire pregnancy, or for a lifetime, I loved this child with all my being.

"I love you," I whispered, through tears. I placed my hand on my belly and said it again. "*I love you.*"

Then I remembered something I'd said to my spiritual director a couple of years before, after one of my miscarriages. "For me, being open to life means being open to death. There's no guarantee I'll carry any baby to term."

I'd realized it before, but I had to learn the lesson again: All that God asks of me is my openness to His will. He will determine the results of my *fiat*s. He will see me through each yes no matter where it takes me. Up the mountaintop or through the valley of grief, He is there.

And so, after all we've been through together, I know that I could trust Him with everything, especially my weakness. As the apostle Paul said, "My grace is sufficient for you, for my power is made perfect in weakness" (2 Corinthians 12:9). God can and will use my weakness for my good and His glory.

Again I shall behold thee, daughter true;
The hour will come when I shall hold thee fast
In God's name, loving thee all through and through.
Somewhere in his grand thought this waits for us.
Then shall I see a smile not like thy last—
For that great thing which came when all was past,
Was not a smile, but God's peace glorious.

—George MacDonald, *Diary of an Old Soul*[8]

. . .

Notes From My Journal

It has happened so slowly. Bit by bit, miscarriage by miscarriage, trust by trust, step by step, I have come to believe that He is in control, that He allows all things for my good. My emotions and fears will rise and fall, but He is over and above them all. They don't rule me. I recognize them for what they are—a part of my broken humanity—but I know that He is the one who rules all things.

> [Wisdom] is a reflection of eternal light,
> a spotless mirror of the working of God,
> and an image of his goodness.
> Though she is but one, she can do all things,

and while remaining in herself, she renews all things;
in every generation she passes into holy souls
and makes them friends of God, and prophets.

—Wisdom 7:26–27

Of Saints, Babies, and Anniversaries

It is the anniversary of the miscarriage of James Matthias. We named him after St. Matthias, on whose feast day he was lost. And that was when I began to pray that James would intercede for his father's faith and conversion. Three months later Tom took his first tentative steps toward Catholicism, and the following year, after my fourth miscarriage, he finally decided he would indeed enter the Church.

Thank you, baby James, and thank you, baby Rachel.

Thank you, God, for the gift of intercessory prayer.

Thank you, Jesus, for our many beautiful children, even if we are able to see and hug and hold only three of them. I know that one magnificent day we will all be together. In the meantime, to my big family in heaven: pray for us!

> Where there is great love there are always miracles.
> —Willa Cather, *Death Comes for the Archbishop*[59]

Presentations

> And a sword will pierce through your own soul.
>
> —Luke 2:35

I've always been struck by the fact that the feast marking Mary's presentation of her Son (the Feast of Candlemas, February 2) also marks her purification, because it has been through the "presentation" of my miscarried children to the Lord that I have been purified, bit by bit and tear by tear.

When I experienced my first miscarriage, I cried to the Lord and asked Him, "Why?"

He whispered in my heart, "I won't tell you why…but I know what you feel." And I was purified, knowing that He's with me in every circumstance and emotion.

When I miscarried again, I asked the Lord, "Will we ever be allowed to have a baby?" and in the depths of my pierced heart I heard Him say that I must walk in darkness for a time. And I was purified, knowing that I do not always understand His ways but that His plans are for my good.

When we followed His promptings to try again but miscarried a third time, I asked the Lord, "How can I trust You again? I was so wrong." He told my confused and grieving heart that I wasn't wrong. He had given us this child. But now He called us to surrender to His wisdom in taking this child so soon. And I was purified, knowing that I could trust His promptings, even when they did not end as I'd hoped they would.

With the next miscarriage I wept to the Lord and said, "I am so sad... but I know You will use this suffering. Please accept it, Lord. I give You my child, and I beg her intercession for her father's sake." And I was purified, knowing that He would allow my children in heaven to pray for their father's conversion.

When I miscarried again, I cried to the Lord, "How I had hoped it would be different this time. I hoped for life instead of death." He held me close and whispered to my bruised and battered heart that my baby did have life, the Life we all long for and hope to share in one day. And in this way He used the life and death of my child to heal me of an old and terrible wound. And I was purified, knowing that He is the Lord of all creation, the Lord of my life, the God who saves and heals me, the Christ.

Mary's *fiat*—her yes—was both openness to life and openness to death, and that is what God has asked of me. To risk life is to risk loss. What choice do I have but to say, "Yes. Let it be done to me according to Your word"?

And so through my *fiat*s He is purifying me—by way of sorrows and swords but also through resurrections. Mary saw her Son again, and I, God willing, will see my children too. Mary's Son and my sons and daughters—Robin, Shelby, James, Rachel, and Raphael—are waiting for me. My presentations, though they carry great suffering, offer me glimpses into the depths of the Divine. I have wept in the nighttime of this life, but there will be joy in the morning (see Psalm 30:5).

Drenched in His Love: Final Notes From My Journal

I kept saying, "Where is God?" as if I expected Jesus to appear before me, take me in His arms, cover me in a sort of divine salve, and dab all my wounds away. That's not exactly how it happened. But so many people did appear. They folded me into their embrace. They held me, listened to me, fed me, shared a glass of wine with me, cried with me, wiped my tears, renewed my hope, resurrected my laughter, and helped to heal my shattered heart.

Who am I to question God's love for me when I've been drenched in His love these last weeks, these months, these years?

> I will lead the blind
>> in a way that they know not,
> in paths that they have not known
>> I will guide them.
> I will turn the darkness before them into light.
>
> . . .

Fear not, for I have redeemed you;
    I have called you by name, you are mine.
When you pass through the waters I will be with you;
    and through the rivers, they shall not overwhelm you;
when you walk through fire you shall not be burned,
    and the flame shall not consume you.
For I am the LORD your God,
    the Holy One of Israel, your Savior.

—Isaiah 42:16, 43:1–3

Notes

1. C.S. Lewis, *A Grief Observed* (1961; New York: Harper and Row, 1989), p. 15.

2. Madeleine L'Engle, *Two-Part Invention: The Story of a Marriage* (New York: Harper and Row, 1989), p. 228.

3. Johnna Miller, e-mail, edited for length and clarity.

4. Emily Dickinson, "Out of the Morning," poem 2 in section 3, "Nature," *Poems: Three Series, Complete*, www.gutenberg.net.

5. From a blog that has gone private.

6. Two Listeners, *God Calling*, ed. A.J. Russell (Old Tappan, N.J.: Spire, 1991), p. 144.

7. Charlotte W., http://tiredtwang.blogspot.com.

8. "R.," e-mail, edited for length and clarity.

9. Francis de Sales, www.oblates.org.

10. Elisabeth, e-mail, edited for length and clarity.

11. Roxane Salonen, originally published at www.catholicmom.com, edited for length.

12. *Book of Blessings* (Collegeville, Minn.: Liturgical, 1992), pp. 95, 99.

13. Aeschylus, as translated by Edith Hamilton in *The Greek Way* (New York: Norton, 1993), p. 61.

14. Sue Umezaki, http://sue-livingandlearning.blogspot.com.

15. William Wordsworth, "Surprised by Joy—Impatient as the Wind," in *Selections from Wordsworth and Tennyson*, ed. Pelham Edgar (Toronto: Macmillan, 1917), at www.gutenberg.net.

16. Karen Murphy Corr, http://busyhandsbc.blogspot.com.

17. Samuel Johnson, "The Proper Means of Regulating Sorrow," in *The Works of Samuel Johnson, With an Essay on His Life and Genius by Arthur Murphy*, vol. 1 (New York: G. Dearborn, 1836), p. 83.

18. Emily Dickinson, "I Many Times Thought Peace Had Come," poem 47 in section 1, "Life," *Poems: Three Series, Complete*, www.gutenberg.net.

19. From a blog that has gone private.

20. William Wordsworth, *Love Letters of William and Mary Wordsworth* (Ithaca, N.Y.: Cornell University Press, 1981), p. 112.

21. Melanie Bettinelli, "The Little Sparrow," www.thewinedarksea.com.

22. Marcel Proust, *Remembrance of Things Past,* vol. 2, trans. C.K. Scott Moncrieff (eBook@Adelaide, 2009), p. 106.

23. Sara Lewis Holmes, "I Could Not Wake You," http://saralewisholmes.blogspot.com.

24. C.S. Lewis, as quoted by Sheldon Vanauken in *A Severe Mercy* (New York: Bantam, 1977), p. 184.

25. E-mail, edited for length.

26. Anthony Beardslee, "Pair of Wings," audio at www.tonybeardslee.com.

27. E-mail, edited for clarity.

28. George MacDonald, *A Book of Strife in the Form of the Diary of an Old Soul*, January 10 (London: Longmans, Green, 1885), www.gutenberg.org.

29. T.S. Eliot, "The Journey of the Magi," *The Waste Land and Other Poems* (New York: Harcourt, Brace and World, 1934), p. 70.

30. Margaret Berns, http://patentsgirl.blogspot.com.

31. Charles de Foucauld, "Prayer of Abandon," extracted from a meditation on the Passion, in *Charles de Foucauld: Journey of the Spirit*, by Cathy Wright (Boston: Pauline, 2005).

32. "B.," e-mail.

33. C.S. Lewis, *A Grief Observed*, pp. 38–39.

34. Ellen Gable Hrkach, ellengable.wordpress.com.

35. Church of the Holy Innocents, www.innocents.com.

36. Janet Brungardt, http//:houseofbrungardt.blogspot.com.

37. L.M. Montgomery, *Anne of the Island: An Anne of Green Gables Story* (1915; New York: Grosset and Dunlap, 1992), p. 213.

38. *Stabat Mater*, found at http://campus.udayton.edu/mary.

39. Josemaría Escrivá, *The Way*, no. 516, in *The Way / Furrow / The Forge* (1939; Princeton, N.J.: Scepter, 1998), p. 125.

40. Augustine, discourse on Psalm 37:13–14, CCL 38, 391–392, as quoted in *The Liturgy of the Hours*, vol. 1 (New York: Catholic Book, 1975), p. 303.

41. Teresa of Avila, "Bookmark," as quoted by Ann Ball in *Encyclopedia of Catholic Devotions and Practices* (Huntington, Ind.: Our Sunday Visitor, 2003), p. 597.

42. Margaret Berns, http://patentsgirl.blogspot.com.

43. Mary DeTurris Poust, http://notstrictlyspiritual.blogspot.com.

44. Julian Stead, as quoted by Vanauken, p. 163.

45. Shushiki, as quoted by Kenneth Yasuda in *The Japanese Haiku: Its Essential Nature, History, and Possibilities in English, with Selected Examples* (White Plains, N.Y.: Peter Pauper, 1958).

46. Jean Pierre de Caussade, as quoted by Martin H. Manser in *The Westminster Collection of Christian Quotations* (Louisville: Westminster John Knox, 2001), p. 156.

47. Willa Cather, *O Pioneers!* (1913; Boston: Houghton Mifflin, 1988), p. 117.

48. Emily Dickinson, "Each That We Lose Takes Part of Us," poem 45 in section 4, "Time and Eternity," *Poems: Three Series, Complete*, www.gutenberg.net.

49. Abigail Benjamin, http://abigails-alcove.blogspot.com.

50. Edward P. Sri, *The New Rosary in Scripture* (Ann Arbor, Mich.: Charis, 2003), pp. 71–72.

51. Alfred Lord Tennyson, "In Memoriam, A.H.H.," stanza 54, in *The Complete Poetical Works of Tennyson* (Cambridge, Mass.: Houghton, Mifflin, 1898), pp. 175–176.

52. Karen Murphy Corr, http://busyhands.blogspot.com.

53. Mary DeTurris Poust, http://notstrictlyspiritual.blogspot.com.

54. Margery Williams, *The Velveteen Rabbit; or, How Toys Become Real* (1922; Tarrytown, N.Y.: Marshall Cavendish, 2011), www.gutenberg.org.

55. Ring Lardner, *The Young Immigrants* (New York: Penguin, 1997), p. 278.

56. Emily Dickinson, "If I Can Stop," poem 51, in in *Poems: Three Series, Complete*, www.gutenberg.net.

57. Thérèse of Lisieux, *Story of a Soul: The Autobiography of St. Thérèse of Lisieux,* trans. John Clarke (Washington, D.C.: ICS, 1976), p. 243.

58. MacDonald, December 29, www.gutenberg.org.

59. Willa Cather, *Death Comes for the Archbishop* (1927; London: Virago, 2008), p. 40.

Resources

Books

Blanford, Cathy R. *Something Happened: A Book for Children and Parents Who Have Experienced Pregnancy Loss.* Self-published, 2008. A picture book from the point of view of a child struggling to understand why there will not be a new baby after all. Most pages also include insets containing information for parents.

DeTurris Poust, Mary. *Parenting a Grieving Child: Helping Children Find Faith, Hope, and Healing After the Loss of a Loved One.* Chicago: Loyola, 2002. Includes a chapter about handling miscarriage with your other children.

Hahn, Kimberly. *Life-Giving Love: Embracing God's Beautiful Design for Marriage.* Ann Arbor: Servant, 2002. This book delves into God's plan for the sacrament of marriage and openness to life, but it also includes a beautiful and helpful chapter about miscarriage and stillbirth.

Kreeft, Peter. *Making Sense Out of Suffering.* Ann Arbor: Charis, 1986. A straightforward, readable book that helps put suffering into a Christian perspective.

L'Engle, Madeleine. *Two-Part Invention: The Story of a Marriage (The Crosswicks Journal, Book 4).* New York: HarperOne, 1989. Written after the death of a spouse, sections of this book help us know we're not alone in the many varied ways of grieving.

Lewis, C.S. *A Grief Observed*. New York: Harper and Row, 1989. Lewis wrote this following the death of his wife, but his descriptions of grief, coping, and healing are universal.

MacDonald, George. *A Book of Strife in the Form of the Diary of an Old Soul*. London: Longmans Green, 1885. Profoundly moving prayers and brief meditations, written after the deaths of two of MacDonald's children.

O'Keeffe Lafser, Christine. *An Empty Cradle, a Full Heart: Reflections for Mothers and Fathers After Miscarriage, Stillbirth, or Infant Death*. Chicago: Loyola, 1998. Brief reflections and accompanying quotes from Scripture, with sections for both mothers and fathers.

Schroeder, Robert G. *John Paul II and the Meaning of Suffering: Lessons From a Spiritual Master*. Huntington, Ind.: Our Sunday Visitor, 2008. A wonderful look at Christian suffering, using the words and work of Blessed John Paul II and his apostolic letter *Salvifici Doloris*. After Schroeder and his wife miscarried their first two children, he discovered John Paul's letter, which helped him on the path to healing.

Articles

Caroline Schermerhorn. "Miscarriage: Moving From Grief Toward Healing." *St. Anthony Messenger*. January 2005. http://americancatholic. org. An excellent and supportive article.

Jeannie Hannemann. "Fertility and Infertility." Elizabeth Ministry International. elizabethministry.com.

Ministries Offering Spiritual and Emotional Support
The Apostolate of Hannah's Tears—http://theapostolateofhannahstears.
blogspot.com/. From its website:

> We offer prayer support and comfort to the brokenhearted who
> suffer the pains of infertility at any stage of life, difficult preg-
> nancy, miscarriage, stillbirth, the loss of a child, and the adoption
> process. This apostolate intercedes for Catholic doctors, nurses,
> and their supportive personnel. We also serve as a vehicle of edu-
> cation in the proper channels of Catholic fertility practices as well
> as offering information resources to those seeking adoption and
> fertility care.

Contact Hannah's Tears, c/o St. Patrick Church, 280 N. Grant Ave.,
Columbus, OH 43215. Prayer requests: Hannahs.Tears.Prayer@gmail.
com. Ministry information: Hannahs.Tears@gmail.com

The Compassionate Friends—www.compassionatefriends.org. A national
support group with local chapters offering grief support after the death of
a child, at any age and from any cause. Visit the website to find a chapter
in your area.

Contact The Compassionate Friends, P.O. Box 3696, Oak Brook, IL
60522. Phone: (877) 969-0010

Elizabeth Ministry International—www.elizabethministry.com. This ministry offers unique and helpful items, such as a miscarriage delivery kit,

which provides "a way to deliver the child with as much dignity as circumstances allow." It also has burial gowns, a tiny burial vessel, and excellent booklets available. Visit the website, click on the online store, and enter "miscarriage" in the search box to locate these resources.

The "Life and Loss Institute" section of the website offers extensive information on issues related to pregnancy and miscarriage, infertility, marriage, natural family planning, and much more, including the teachings of the Catholic Church on these issues.

Contact Elizabeth Ministry International, 120 W. 8th St., Kaukauna, WI 54130. Phone: (920) 766-9380

Morning Light Ministry—www.morninglightministry.org. Free prayer cards are offered to all bereaved parents, siblings, and grandparents. Many other resources, ideas for support, and free phone support, are available from this Catholic group.

Share Pregnancy and Infant Loss Support, Inc.—www.nationalshare.org. From its website:

> The mission of Share Pregnancy and Infant Loss Support, Inc. is to serve those whose lives are touched by the tragic death of a baby through early pregnancy loss, stillbirth, or in the first few months of life.

Share offers a wide range of support ideas and resources, twenty-four-hour telephone support, an online chat room, and help with locating local support groups.

Contact Share Pregnancy and Infant Loss Support, Inc., 402 Jackson St., St. Charles, MO 63301. Phone: (636) 947-6164 or (800) 821-6819

Blogs

Please visit the blogs of some of the women who contributed to this book:

Abigail Benjamin, Abigail's Alcove (abigails-alcove.blogspot.com)

Margaret Berns, Minnesota Mom (patentsgirl.blogspot.com)

Melanie Bettinelli, The Wine Dark Sea (thewinedarksea.com)

Janet Brungardt, House of Brungardt (houseofbrungardt.blogspot.com)

Mary DeTurris Poust, Not Strictly Spiritual (notstrictlyspiritual.blogspot. com)

Ellen Gable Hrkach, Plot Line and Sinker (ellengable.wordpress.com)

Sara Lewis Holmes, Read Write Believe (saralewisholmes.blogspot.com)

Karen Murphy Corr, Busy Hands (busyhandsbc.blogspot.com)

Roxane Salonen, Peace Garden Mama (roxanesalonen.blogspot.com)

Sue Umezaki, Living and Learning (sue-livingandlearning.blogspot.com)

Charlotte W., Waltzing Matilda (tiredtwang.blogspot.com)

Memorial Items and Keepsakes

Rosaries With Names—www.rosarieswithnames.com. Handmade, personalized rosaries, chaplets, prayer bracelets, and sacrifice beads. You can specify the name or names of your loved ones to be imprinted on the rosary beads (not limited to five decades).

Contact Chris Lafser, P.O. Box 8223, Richmond, VA 23226. Phone: (804) 358-6104

Shrine of the Holy Innocents—www.innocents.com/shrine. A beautiful memorial to unborn children at the Church of the Holy Innocents. Visit the shrine's website to add your baby's name to "The Book of Life." You may also request a certificate (printable email attachment) in honor of your child. Contact Church of the Holy Innocents, 128 W. 37th St., New York, NY 10018. Phone: (212) 279-5861

Memorial Cards

Personalize the prayer card of your choice as a remembrance of your child. Available from the Catholic Company (www.catholiccompany.com), Customized Catholic Prayer Cards (www.customizedcatholicprayercards. net), Aquinas and More Catholic Goods (www.aquinasandmore.com). Or check with your favorite Catholic book or gift store.

Ask your priest if your diocese offers prayer cards or other memorial items.

Memory Books

Gordon, Russ, and June Gordon. *Forever in Our Hearts.* An album with space for keepsakes, journaling, and pictures. Available through Share Pregnancy and Infant Loss Support, Inc. Visit www.stores.nationalshare. org and search the catalog for the title.

In the Company of Angels. Austin: Casey Shay, 2010. A lovely memorial book for your baby. You can see the entire contents of the book on a video at www.caseyshaypress.com.

Medical Resources

One More Soul—www.onemoresoul.com. Medical resources, listings of pro-life and NFP (natural family planning) doctors.

Pope Paul VI Institute—www.popepaulVI.com. Extensive information, services, and links on fertility care and women's health, "fostering God's plan for love, chastity, marriage, and children."

Index of "Did You Know?" Topics

Printed in the United States
By Bookmasters